Sweet & Sour

The Royal Critic

We cannot bear to roast a book,
    Nor brutally attack it;
We lay it gently on our lap
    And dust its little jacket.

KEITH PRESTON

The Fisherman who cannot wait
reels in his line and eats the bait.

LIBBY HOUSTON

Sweet & Sour
An Anthology of Comic Verse

Edited by
Christopher Logue

Illustrations by John Glashan

Come hither, idiot reader,
And you shall have today
A pennyworth of poppycock
To pass the time away.

J.B. MORTON

B.T. Batsford Ltd, London.

by the same author

Ode to the Dodo, Poems from 1953 to 1978 (Cape),
War Music (Cape)
The Bumper Book of True Stories, Private Eye
(André Deutsch)
The Children's Book of Comic Verse (Batsford)

Two wrongs won't make a right: the odds are long
That two rights, though, will make at least one wrong.

BIAS OF PRIENE TRANSLATED BY L. A. MACKAY

First published 1983
© Christopher Logue

ISBN 0 7134 3792 8

Printed in Great Britain
by Biddles Ltd
Guildford, Surrey
for the publishers,
B T Batsford Ltd,
4 Fitzhardinge Street,
London, W1H 0AH

for Bernard Stone

I seen a dunce of a poet once, a writin' a little book;
And he says to me with a smile, says he,
"Here's a pome – d'you want to look?"
And I threw me eye at the pome; say I,
"What's the use o' this here rot?"
"It's a double sestine," says he, lookin' mean,
"And they're hard as the deuce, that's what!"

GELETT BURGESS

To the Reader

Afore ye take in hand this beuk
To these few lines jist gie a leuk.
Be sure that baith ye'r hands are clean,
Sic as are fitten to be seen,
Free fra a' dirt, an' black coal coom;
Fra ash-hole dust, an' chimley bloom;
O' creesh fra candle or fra lamp,
Upon it leave nae filthy stamp.
I'd rather gie a siller croon,
Than see a butter'd finger'd loon,
Wi' parritch, reemin fra his chaps,
Fast fa'in down in slav'rin draps
Upon the beuk. Hech! for each sowp,
I'd wish a nettle in his doup
For every creeshie drap transparent,
I'd wish his neck wi' a sair hair in't:
Sic plague spots on ilk bonnie page,
Wad mak a sant e'en stamp wi' rage.
    Reader, ye'll no tak amiss,
Sic an impertinence as this:
Ye'r no the ane that e'er wad do't –
An use a beuk like an old cloot;
Ye wadn wi' y'er fingers soil it –
Nor creesh, no blot, not rend, nor spoil it.

ANONYMOUS

Contents

Ready to perform at a poetry reading, my impatience with the endless blather of those on stage was calmed when one who waited beside me, wrote:

Bernard Kops
never stops.
He is Jeremy Robson
with knobs on.

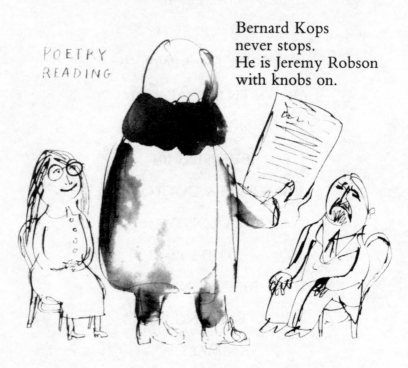

POETRY READING

When I had my operation
I displayed a lot of guts,
I could take it, smile, and like it,
But the bed-pan drove me nuts.

Preface

Thy drasty rhyming is not worth a turd.

Geoffrey Chaucer

Introduction

There is pleasure in teasing one's betters: hence, two pieces of fool's gold:

from *Chaucer*

    A joking bard, whose antiquated muse
    In mouldy words could solid sense produce

SAMUEL COBB

and from *On Chaucer*

    No doubt he well invented – nobly felt –
    But O ye Powers! how monstrously he spelt.

HARTLEY COLERIDGE

Replying to a letter of mine about the contents of this book, Stanley J. Sharpless wrote: *'Cocoa' has been my most anthologised piece. I don't know whether you'd consider that a reason for putting it in or leaving it out.*
'As you, Mr Sharpless,' I said to myself, 'have pieces as good as "Cocoa", I shall leave it out,' for as far as I have been able to do so my aim had been to avoid often anthologised pieces, and to accept the risk foreseen by Arthur Guitterman:

    Since one anthologist put in his book
    Sweet things by More, Bone, Potter, Bliss and Brook,
    All subsequent anthologists, of course,
    Have quoted Bliss, Brook, Potter, Bone and Morse.
    For, should some rash anthologist make free
    To print selections, say, from you and me,

Omitting with a judgement all his own
The classic Brook, Morse, Potter, Bliss and Bone,
Contemptuous reviewers, passing by
Our verses, would unanimously cry,
'What manner of anthology is this
That leaves out Bone, Brook, Potter, Morse and Bliss!'

While there must be something to the murmur that the
value of *Sweet and Sour* has been reduced by the
omission of certain famous authors, ordinary readers
who, for the most part, get their poetry from
anthologies have only to turn to the list of Books
Consulted and they will find titles thick with items by
Morse, Potter, Bliss and Co.

O you! whom vanity's light bark conveys
On fame's mad voyage by the wind of praise;
With what a shifting gale your course you ply;
For ever sunk too low, or born too high!
Who pants for glory finds but short repose,
A breath revives him, or a breath o'erthrows!

Among the most enjoyable of an anthologist's decisions
is who to leave out and thereafter to chose which excuse
to give to which long face. 'Ah, my dear Trumbull, you
are at your best in your longer poems, and there was
simply not enough space.' 'Your Permission Fees, Miss
Scram, are not in line with Government policy for the
lower paid.' 'But you are already an author of
international repute, Mr Toadpool.' 'Never mind,
Growser, I omitted Shakespeare, too.'

11

That long straight vest, and that unmanly ruffle,
In our opinion form a curious muffle.
Much better wouldst thou look if thou was clad
In MOSES' matchless dress, thou clever lad.

MOSES & SON, TAILORS, ALDGATE

To strike a historical note: at least as much good comic verse exists in English as good verse of any other kind; collections of such verse have been published since the 1650s; and most of these anthologies mix the sweet and the sour. This, from *Le Prince d'Amour* (1660) of the former kind:

An Old Courtier

An old song made by an old aged pate,
Of an old worshipful gentleman had a wealthy estate,
That kept an old house at a bountiful rate,
And an old Porter to relieve poor people at his gate,
    Like an old Courtier of the Queens,
    And the Queens old Courtier.

With an old Lady whose anger one word asswageth,
Who ever quarter paid his old servants their wages,
Who never knew what belonged to Coachman, Footmen
  nor Pages,
But kept two and fifty men in blew caps and badges.
  Like an old courtier...

With an old studdy stuft full of old learned books,
And old Parson, you may know him by his old looks;
With an old buttry hatch worn quite off the old hooks,
An old kitchin that maintain'd half a dozen old Cooks.
  Like an old...

With an old hall hung with pikes, guns and bows,
And old blades and bucklers had born many shrewd blows,
With an old freezadoe coat to cover his drunck hose,
With an old cup of sherry to comfort his old nose.
  Like an old...

With an old fashion when Christmas was come,
To call in all his old neighbors with a bagpipe or a drum,
And good cheer enough to furnish out every old room,
And beer and ale would make a cat speak, and a wise man
dumb.
  Like an old...

With an old faulkner, a huntsman, and a kennel of hounds,
That never hauked nor hunted but in his grandfathers old
  grounds,
Who like a wiseman kept himself in his own old bounds,
And when he died gave each child a thousand old pounds.
  Like an old...

ANONYMOUS

13

and these, from *Wit and Drollery* and *Choice Drollery (both 1656) of the latter:*

On Her Husband

His beard is much like rusty wire,
His pimples black as tow,
His lips like parchment curled by fire,
His forehead wondrous low.

His squinting, staring, goggling eyes
Poor children to affright,
His nose is double Roman size
And sheds a purple light.

His oven-mouth wide open stands,
With teeth like rotten peas;
His brick-dust neck, his flour-sack hands,
His chest all bit with fleas.

His ears might draw a galleon,
His belly holds a rick,
No roasted ox can match his bum
For broadness, fat and thick.

Thus have you heard my husband praised,
And yet no flattery used;
Pray tell me, is he not of worth?
Let him not be abused.

ANONYMOUS

14

On His Wife

No gipsy nor no blackamoor,
No Bloomsbury nor Tyburn whore,
Can half so black, so foul appear,
As she I chose to be my dear.
She's wrinkled, old, she's dry, she's tough,
Yet money makes her fair enough.

ANONYMOUS

Because *Sweet and Sour* is meant for your amusement I have, as with the pair above, modernised some of its poems. Should scholars feel the need to complain, let me remind them that they are entirely responsible for any mistakes that occur in the unedited poems, and by the way of compensation suggest that they memorise the following couplet:

On a Certain Scholar

He never completed his History of Ephesus,
But his name got mentioned in numerous prefaces.

W. CRADDLE

Singles

'Go tell your tale, Lord Lovell.' she said,
'To the maritime cavalree,
To your grandmother of the hoary head –
To any one but me...'

ANONYMOUS

Späcially Jim

I wus mighty good-lookin' when I wus young,
  Peert an' black-eyed an' slim,
With fellers a-courtin' me Sunday nights,
  'Späcially Jim.

The likeliest one of 'em all wus he,
  Clipper an' han'som' an' trim;
But I tossed up my head an' made fun o' the crowd,
  'Späcially Jim.

I said I hadn't no 'pinion o' men,
  An' I wouldn't take stock in him!
But they kep' on a-comin in spite o' my talk,
  'Späcially Jim.

I got so tired o' having' 'em roun'
  ('Späcially Jim!)
I made up my mind I'd settle down
  An' take up with him.

So we wus married one Sunday in church,
  'Twas crowded full to the brim;
'Twas the only way to git rid of 'em all,
  'Späcially Jim.

ANONYMOUS

The Expense of Spirits
Is a Crying Shame

The expense of spirits is a crying shame;
So is the cost of wine. What bard today
Can live like old Khayyam? It's not the same –
A loaf and Thou and Tesco's beaujolais.
I had this bird called Sharon, fond of gin –
Could knock back six or seven. At the price,
I paid a high wage for each hour of sin
And that was why I only had her twice.
Then there was Tracy, who drank rum and coke –
So beautiful I didn't mind at first
But love grows colder. Now some other bloke
Is subsidising Tracy and her thirst.
I need a woman, honest and sincere,
Who'll come across on half a pint of beer.

WENDY COPE

18

My Rival

I go to concert, party, ball –
   What profit is in these?
I sit alone against the wall
   And strive to look at ease.
The incense that is mine by right
   They burn before Her shrine;
And that's because I'm seventeen.
   And she is forty-nine.

She calls me 'darling', 'pet', and 'dear',
   And 'sweet retiring maid'.
I'm always at the back, I know –
   She puts me in the shade.
She introduces me to men –
   'Cast' lovers, I opine;
For sixty takes to seventeen,
   Nineteen to forty-nine.

But even She must older grow
   And end Her dancing days,
She can't go on for ever so
   At concerts, balls and plays.
One ray of priceless hope I see
   Before my footsteps shine;
Just think, that She'll be eighty-one
   When I am forty-nine!

RUDYARD KIPLING

Ludmilla

Ludmilla, the Soviet lassie,
  Has many a notch in her gun;
She thinks it a trifle to pick up a rifle
  And blow out the brains of a Hun.
If cartridges happen to fail her,
  She's equally expert with steel;
She uses a dagger to cut off the swagger
  Of ev'ry Hilterian heel.

The Finns and Rumanians dread her;
  Their leader has only to cry;
'Ach, here comes Ludmilla, the demon guerrilla.'
  And back to their bases they fly.
Contrariwise, Russians adore her –
  The gal with the gat in her gown;
From Omsk to Tiflis the redoubtable miss
  Is toasted by country and town.

But where is the Muscovite hero
  Would venture Ludmilla to date?
Her great reputation for swift liquidation
  Would make her a perilous mate.
One man, and one only, is worthy;
  I move, Mr. Chief Commissar –
And the motion is carried – that she shall be married
  To Ivan Skavinsky Skavar.

ERNEST W. THIELE

To James Who Could Not Suffer Fools Gladly

Suffer fools as best you can:
You would be a lonely man,
James, if every fool you knew
Found he could not suffer you.

COLIN ELLIS

A Slice of Wedding Cake

Why have such scores of lovely, gifted girls
   Married impossible men?
Simple self-sacrifice may be ruled out,
   And missionary endeavour, nine times out of ten.

Repeat 'impossible men' – not merely rustic
   Foul-tempered, or depraved
(Dramatic foils chosen to show the world
   How well women behave, and always have behaved).

Impossible men, idle, illiterate,
   Self-pitying, dirty, sly,
For whose appearance even in City parks
   Excuses must be made to casual passers-by.

Has God's supply of tolerable husbands
   Fallen, in fact, so low?
Or do I always over-value woman
   At the expense of man?
               Do I?
                    It might be so.

ROBERT GRAVES

Take Me in Your Arms, Miss Moneypenny-Wilson

Take me in your arms, Miss Moneypenny-Wilson,
　Take me in your arms, Miss Bates;
Fatal are your charms, Miss Moneypenny-Wilson,
　Fatal are your charms, Miss Bates;
Say you are my own, Miss Moneypenny-Wilson,
　Say you are my own, Miss Bates;
You I love alone, Miss Moneypenny-Wilson,
　You, and you alone, Miss Bates.

Sweet is the morn, Miss Moneypenny-Wilson;
　Sweet is the dawn, Miss B.,
But sweeter than the dawn and the daisies on the lawn
　Are you, sweet nymphs, to me.
Sweet, sweet, sweet is the sugar to the beet,
　Sweet is the honey to the bee,
But sweeter far than such sweets are
　Are your sweet names to me.

Deaf to my cries, Miss Moneypenny-Wilson,
　Deaf to my sighs, Miss B.,
Deaf to my songs and the story of my wrongs,
　Deaf to my minstrelsy;
Deafer than the newt to the sound of a flute,
　Deafer than a stone to the sea;
Deafer than a heifer to the sighing of a zephyr
　Are your deaf ears to me.

Cold, cold, cold as the melancholy mould,
   Cold as the foam-cold sea,
Colder than the shoulder of a neolithic boulder
   Are the shoulders you show to me.
Cruel, cruel, cruel is the flame to the fuel,
   Cruel is the axe to the tree,
But crueller and keener than a coster's concertina
   Is your cruel, cruel scorn to me.

PATRICK BARRINGTON

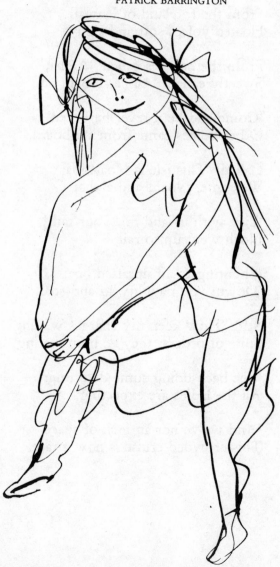

Noah

After all the flood-storm's dark
A southern sun shone on the ark.

From the foreland of Hawaii
Floated voices soft and sighy,

From the beaches called: 'Aloha,'
Sweetly called: 'Aloha, Noah,

'Come and be forever harbored'
Other voices came from starboard,

Called: 'This isle is Noa-Noa;
Welcome, Noah, and aloha;

'Live with us and furl your sail.'
Noah went up to rail,

(Shouting to an upraised boa:
'Down! you naughty so-and-soa!)

Said: 'How keep my charges waiting?
Spite of orders, they've been mating.

'I've been doing some detecting;
All the ladies are expecting;

'And we've not an inch of space.
This crowded cruise is now a race.

'I must get my charges home,
Have no time for even Rome;

'And you're all so loving here.'
Noah turned to hide a tear;

Said: 'The answer must be noa.
I am Noah; I must goa.'

So he left the siren seas,
Left the luring melodies,

Left the loving maidens flat;
Ran aground on Ararat.

O those islands! O those seas!
O those siren melodies!

Hark! I hear that sweet Aloha.
Am I yes or am I Noah?

CLARK STILLMAN

Wind and Water

Old Noah he had an ostrich farm and fowls on the largest
   scale,
He ate his egg with a ladle in an egg-cup as big as a pail,
And the soup he took was Elephant Soup and the fish he
   took was Whale,
But they all were small to the cellar he took when he set
   out to sail,
And Noah he often said to his wife when they sat down to
   dine,
'I don't care where the water goes if it doesn't get into the
   wine.'

The cataract of the cliff of heaven fell blinding off the
   brink
As if it would wash the stars away as suds go down a sink,
The seven heavens came roaring down the throats of hell
   to drink,
And Noah he cocked his eye and said 'It looks like rain, I
   think,
The water has drowned the Matterhorn as deep as a
   Mendip mine,
But I don't care where the water goes if it doesn't get into
   the wine.'

But Noah he sinned, and we have sinned, on tipsy feet we
   trod,
Till a great big black teetotaller was sent to us for a rod,
And you can't get wine at a P.S.A., or chapel, or
   Eisteddfod,
For the Curse of Water has come again because of the
   wrath of God,
And water is on the Bishop's board and the Higher
   Thinker's shrine,
But I don't care where the water goes if it doesn't get into
   the wine.

G.K. CHESTERTON

From Noah to Now

In the days of Father Noah life was sweet – life was sweet.
  He played the soft majubal every day.
And for centuries and centuries he never crossed the street,
  Much less supposed he'd ever move away.
But times grew bad and men grew bad, all up and down
    the land,
  And the soft majubal got all out of key;
And when the weather changed, besides, 'twas more than
    he could stand.
  So Father Noah he packed and put to sea.

And 'Yo-ho-ho,' with a mournful howl, said the poor old
    boy to Ham;
  And 'Yo-ho-ho,' sang Japhet, and a pink but tuneful
    clam;
And 'Yo-ho-ho,' cried the sheep, and Shem, and a pair of
    protozoa:
'We're a-going to roam till we find a home that will suit
    old Father Noah.'

                                        CLARENCE DAY

Matrimony

T.99 would gladly hear
  From one whose years are few –
A maid whose doctrines are severe
  Of Presbyterian blue,
Also – with view to the above –
  Her photo he would see,
And trusts that she may live and love
  His Protestant to be!
But ere that sacred rites are done
  (And by no priest of Rome)
He'd ask if she a Remington
  Type-writer works – at home
If she have no objections to
  This task, and if her hair –
In keeping with her eyes of blue –
  Be delicately fair;
Ah, then let her a photo send
  Of all her charms divine,
To him who rests her faithful friend,
  Her own T.99.

ANDREW LANG

It Was Not Much, But It Was Something

When I am dead
I should like this to be said
above my coffin :

she would endeavour
while walking never
to take precedence
over an ambulance
at a zebra crossing

LIBBY HOUSTON

Liberty Preserved

At length the bondage I have broke
  Which gave me so much pain;
I've slipt my heart out of the yoke,
  Never to drudge again;
And, conscious of my long disgrace,
  Have thrown my chain at Cupid's face.

If ever he attempt again
  My freedom to enslave,
I'll court the Godhead of champagne
  Which makes the coward brave;
And, when that deity has heal'd my soul,
  I'll drown the little Bastard in my bowl.

ALEXANDER ROBERTSON OF STRUAN

A Friendly Soul

He's a friendly soul and he longs to please;
   His sins, he is sure, are venial;
   And he's trying to put her quite at her ease
By being extremely genial.
   She does seem cold,
   But he means no harm.
   His jokes are old
   But his heart is warm.
So he clacks his tongue and he racks his brain,
And her sniffs and snubs are all in vain.

CLARENCE DAY

I Can't Think What he Sees in Her

Jealousy's an awful thing and foreign to my nature;
I'd punish it by law if I was in the Legislature.
One can't have all of any one, and wanting it is mean
But still, there is a limit, and I speak of Miss Duveen.

I'm not a jealous woman,
     But I can't see what he sees in her,
       I can't see what he sees in her,
         I can't see what he sees in her!
If she was something striking
I could understand the liking
And I wouldn't have a word to say to that;
     But I can't see why he's fond
     Of that objectionable blonde –
That fluffy little, stuffy little, trashy little,
     creepy-crawly, music-hally, horrid little CAT!

I wouldn't say a word against the girl – be sure of that;
It's not the creature's fault she has the manners of a rat.
Her dresses may be dowdy, but her hair is always new,
And if she squints a little bit – well, many people do.

I'm not a jealous woman,
     But I can't see what he sees in her,
       I can't see what he sees in her,
         I can't see what he sees in her!
He's absolutely free –
There's no bitterness in me,
Though an ordinary woman would explode;
     I'd only like to know
     What he sees in such a crow
As that insinuating, calculating, irritating, titivating,
     sleepy little, creepy little, sticky little TOAD!

A. P. HERBERT

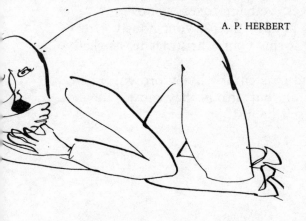

Answer to a Letter from The Hon. Mrs Pole Carew,

in which she had said:
'I am very happy, and care every day less for poetry
and painting, and more for cookery and poultry' – From
ANTONY.

Blest be the day that on your book of life
Stamp't the fair title of a happy wife!
Blest be the hand that, arm'd with virtuous rage,
Tore thence, or cancell'd, every useless page,
Renounc'd the pomps of vanities and wit,
Poultry inscribed where Poetry was writ,
Painting (unprofitable art) effaced,
And gave to Cookery all your thoughts on taste;
Who deck those altars, feed no transient flame,
Nor solid pudding change for empty fame.
May each revolving year your joys increase,
With added flocks of guinea fowls and geese;
On countless eggs may ducks and pigeons sit!
And all attain the honours of the spit!
Chickens in multitudes be hatch'd, and oh!
May no chill autumn lay your turkies low;
Their tender lives, ye felon foxes, spare!
Make them, ye poultry maids, your hourly care!
So their plump forms your Christmas feasts shall
crown,
Well trussed and roasted of a lively brown;
Boiling is spoiling; but, if boil they must,
To insipidity itself be just.

O'er their pale limbs be creamy currants pour'd,
And the rich sauce stand plenteous on your board;
See round your shores th' instructive lesson float,
Within the oyster, and without the boat;
Nor make your sauce so thin, no half so salt.

Happy, whom thus domestic pleasures fix,
Blest with one husband, and with many chicks.

CATHERINE MARIA FANSHAWE

Jane

'If that's what they call worse than death,'
Said Jane, supine on the settee,
'There'll be no moaning at the bar
When I put out to sea.'

STANLEY J. SHARPLESS

Girls

Girls! although I am a woman
I always try to appear human

Unlike Miss So-and-So whose greatest pride
Is to remain always in the VI Form and not let down the side

Do not sell the pass dear, dont let down the side
That is what this woman said and a lot of balsy stuff beside
(Oh the awful balsy nonsense that this woman cried.)

Girls! I will let down the side if I get a chance
And I will sell the pass for a couple of pence.

STEVIE SMITH

Who and What

Who drags the fiery artist down?
What keeps the pioneer in town?
Who hates to let the seaman roam?
It is the wife, it is the home.

CLARENCE DAY

Abracadabra

Look on me with favour, sweet,
And you'll have me at your feet.

Turn the other way, and you'll
Find me every bit as cool.

Here's the secret of my peace:
I can love, and I can cease

Loving, too, if I am not
Noticed, darling, quite a lot.

MARGARET FISHBACK

Vive le Roi

Grief at the Loved One's parting from this Life
Is doubled for the ill-provided Wife.
With more Philosophy the Widow bears
That Husband's Loss, who leaves behind some Shares.
Life's Continuity demands this so:
The Breadwinner is dead – long live the Dough!

JUSTIN RICHARDSON

Moody

I thirst for thirstiness, I weep for tears;
Well pleased I am to be displeased thus;
The only thing I fear is want of fears;
Suspecting, I am not suspicious.
   I cannot choose but live, because I die,
    And when I am not dead how glad am I.

Yet when I am thus glad for sense of pain
And careless am lest I should careless be,
Then do I grieve for being glad again,
And fear lest carelessness take care of me.
   Amid these restless thoughts, this rest I find,
   For those that rest not here there's rest behind.

THOMAS GATAKER

Rufus

Let Rufus weep, rejoice, stand, sit, or walk,
Still he can nothing but of Naevia talk;
Let him eat, drink, ask questions, or dispute,
Still he must speak of Naevia, or be mute,
He writ to his father, ending with this line,
'I am, my lovely Naevia, ever thine.'

MARTIAL TRANSLATED BY RICHARD STEELE

Couples

After the Wedding

Be plain in dress, and sober in your diet;
In short, my Dearie – kiss me, and be quiet.

LADY MARY WORTLEY MONTAGU

News Item

Men seldom make passes
At girls who wear glasses.

DOROTHY PARKER

But safety pins and bassinets
Await the girl who fascinets.

OGDEN NASH

Question and Answer

Why don't the men propose mama
What keeps them all at bay
Where are the local beaux mama
Why do they shy away?

Where does it all go wrong mama
Why is the outlook bleak
Do I come on too strong mama
Is it my poor technique?

Why should they all take fright mama
Why do they leave me flat
Am I such dynamite mama
Please, can you answer that?

'My darling, you're coming up twenty four
And it's getting beyond a joke,
I've told you a thousand times before...
IT'S BECAUSE YOU'RE A BLEEDIN' BLOKE!'

J. J. WEBSTER

Punch and Judy Show

Bastard and Bitch lived in a house,
One had a grudge, the other a grouse;
Grouse and Grudge lived side by side,
Though doors and windows were open wide.

Was it sex, that cur, that kept them together?
Or the visibly querulous weather?
Lethargy, was it? or expectation
That through their front door would walk Salvation,

Goodlooking, impeccable, endlessly kind,
To make off with Himher, leaving Herhim behind?
Acrimonious fidelity is not so uncommon,
Time grieved them grey, the man and the woman;-

Knocker and Scold, knocked out, made hoarse,
And the onlookers well-entertained of course.
Fold up the booth, pack in the scene,
The moon comes out, and the tide flows in.

GERDA MAYER

48

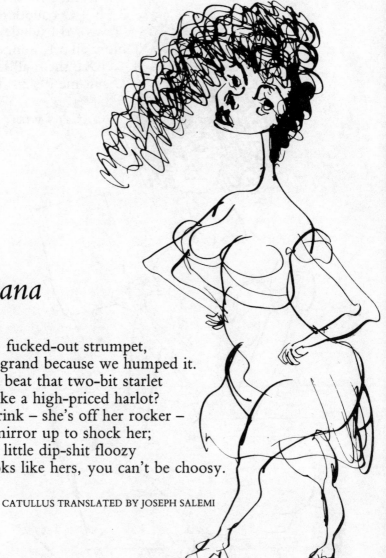

Ameana

Ameana, fucked-out strumpet,
Wants a grand because we humped it.
Can you beat that two-bit starlet
Acting like a high-priced harlot?
Get a shrink – she's off her rocker –
Hold a mirror up to shock her;
Tell that little dip-shit floozy
With looks like hers, you can't be choosy.

CATULLUS TRANSLATED BY JOSEPH SALEMI

A Proposal

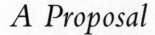

O FE dear, what XTC
I MN8 when U IC!
Once KT 1 me with her I's;
2 LN I O countless sighs.
'Twas MLE while over Cs.
Now all 3 R nonNTTs,
4 U XL them all U C
U suit me FE 2 a T.

LOUISE J. WALKER

Life from a Goldfish Bowl

Mr Murple called upon his mother
Bringing a bottle of gin for Mother's Day;
They tolerate, indeed they love each other
And often rub each other the right way.
'Mother,' he said, 'I brought you this here gin,
Product of Messrs Moult, Moultville, you know.
Look at the fancy piece of glass it's in!
Times have been extra good to Moult and Co.'

'Drat the flies, they're awful bad this year!'
She said, waving a big one from her nose.
'What have you got there? Bless your heart, my dear!
Put it on the piano, by the rose.
A nice red rose to show I'm still alive:
Fifty cents they asked me for it, thieves!
Yellow to show you're dead is fifty-five
All done up in ferny things and leaves.'

What a life for a goldfish, day and night
Who fins in Mr. Murple's mother's bowl!
He gets a bit of flat stuff for a bite
Maybe, or maybe ant eggs – eaten whole –
And notes the goings-on with goggle face
Of all the world around about in air:
Of Mr. Murple with his gloves and grace
Coming with gifts for mother in her lair.

GEORGE JOHNSTON

Autumn

He told his life story to Mrs Courtly
Who was a widow. 'Let us get married shortly',
He said, 'I am no longer passionate,
But we can have some conversation before it is too, late.'

STEVIE SMITH

Song

Pious Selinda goes to prayers,
    If I but ask a favour;
And yet the tender fool's in tears,
    When she believes I'll leave her.

Would I were free from this restraint,
    Or else had hope to win her!
Would she could make of me a saint,
    Or I of her a sinner!

WILLIAM CONGREVE

The Tides of Love

Flo was fond of Ebenezer –
'Eb', for short, she called her beau,
Talk of Tides of Love, great Caesar!
You should see them – Eb and Flo.

T.A.DALY

40 – love

middle	aged
couple	playing
ten	nis
when	the
game	ends
and	they
go	home
the	net
will	still
be	be
tween	them

RODGER MCGOUGH

The Act

(Words for music)

There was a burly mare
Whose rider was a clown
And when he danced upon her
She tossed him up and down:

Halloo, halloo, what merriment,
She tossed him up and down.

They bounded, he on her,
All in the ring of pleasure,
She trotted well, that old grey mare,
He jigged a cheerful measure.

Halloo, halloo, what merriment,
He jigged a cheerful measure.

GERDA MAYER

On the Angel at Basinstoke

When Hope and Prudence kept this House,
An Angel kept the door.
Now Hope is dead,
The Angel fled,
And Prudence turned a whore.

The Angel was kept by Mrs Hope and her daughter, Prudence.
Ben Jonson is said to have composed the rhyme.

Church & State

The gates of Fame are open wide
Its halls are always full,
And some go in by the door marked Push
And some by the door marked Pull.

ANONYMOUS

Ode on Mr John Burns

Who, after being a pro-feminist, voted against female
suffrage because a militant lady threw a pot of
chrysanthemums at him at a flower show.

He was once as he said in the ranks of our friends and I
    think that we trusted him then,
He was anxious to serve our political ends (but you
    cannot be certain with Men).
Now he leaves us and goes to the side of our foes, and I
    ask you tell me for what?
Why, in speaking (forsooth!) he was hit on the nose by
    a single chrysanthemum pot!
Sure a liberal mind must discern the intent of the
    militant lady who threw,
It was obviously meant as a hint of dissent and a partial
    divergence of view
He had only to own he had spoken amiss and
    acknowledge his proneness to err,
I am perfectly sure that expressions like this would
    completely have satisfied her!
When a speaker is struck by an egg or a stone or the
    mortal remains of a cat,
He has cause to complain, I am willing to own, and I
    would not condemn him for that;
But there's nothing at all in chrysanthemum pots that is
    other than proper and fair,
They are simply a part of the several lots which we all
    are expected to bear.

A. D. GODLEY

Holy Scripture

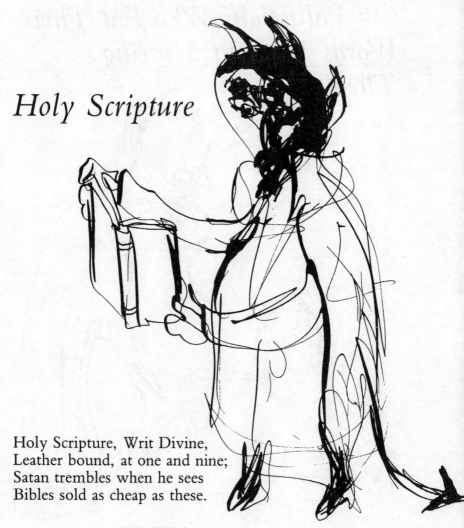

Holy Scripture, Writ Divine,
Leather bound, at one and nine;
Satan trembles when he sees
Bibles sold as cheap as these.

ANONYMOUS

On Politicians Who Eat Their Words Without Mincing Them.

'He does not mince his words!' you cry;
    Yet 'tis an open question
If candour bold and courage high
    Conduce to good digestion;
No; caution points the Statesman's way,
    'Twill save him pain and sorrow
To think that he has minced to-day
    What he must eat to-morrow.

A. D. GODLEY

58

Low Church

It was after vespers one evening
When the vicar, inflamed by desire,
Beckoned a lad to the vestry,
Dismissing the rest of the choir.

He said, 'I've got something to show you,'
The boy followed hard on his heels,
Behind the locked door there was silence,
Except for some half-muffled squeals.

The vicar got two years (suspended),
The judge spoke of 'moral decay',
The vicar is sadder and wiser,
But the choir-boy is happy and gay.

STANLEY J. SHARPLESS

Brébeuf and His Brethren

When Lallemant and de Brébeuf, brave souls,
Were dying by the slow and dreadful coals
Their brother Jesuits in France and Spain
Were burning heretics with equal pain.

F.R. SCOTT

Mr Bruce

Written in Harrow Churchyard on the occasion of a wedding being delayed by the absence of the officiating minister.

Mr Bruce, Mr Bruce,
　　　When the matrimonial noose
You ought here at Harrow to be tying,
　　　If you choose to ride away
　　　As you know you did to-day,
No wonder bride and bridegroom should be crying.
　　　It's a very great abuse,
　　　　Mr Bruce, Mr Bruce!
　　　And you're quite without excuse,
　　　　And of very little use
　　　　　As a curate,
　　　　　　Mr Bruce!

R.H. BARHAM

Knox

O Knox he was a bad man
he split the Scottish mind.
The one half he made cruel
and the other half unkind.
As for you, as for you, as for you, auld Jesus lad,
gawn dance the nails fae oot yer taes, an try an be
　　mair glad.

ALAN JACKSON

60

Chimpanzee

A talented young chimpanzee
Was keen to appear on TV.
He wrote to Brooke Bond
But they didn't respond
So he had to become an MP.

WENDY COPE

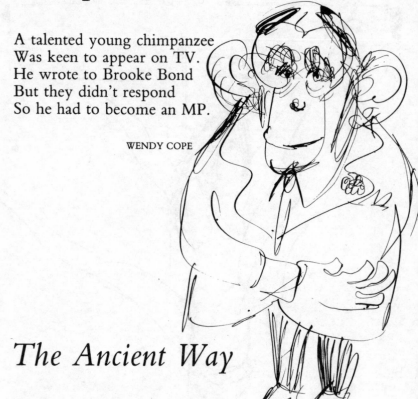

The Ancient Way

'Accept, O God,' said Abraham,
'My son instead of ram or lamb.
At Thy command I've brought my knife
To sacrifice young Isaac's life.'
God smiles, ''Tis well, good Abraham!
But this time I will take the ram.'

In many a kindlier era since,
This tale has made boys' fathers wince....
    Yet when the God of War feels gory,
Even today, do fathers falter?
    No – like old Abraham in the story
They lay their sons upon the altar.

CLARENCE DAY

The Annexation of Natal
August 8, 1843

When we in touch with heathens come,
We send them first a case of rum,
Next, to rebuke their native sin,
We send a missionary in:
Then when the hungry Hottentot
Has boiled his pastor in a pot,
We teach him Christian, dumb contrition
By means of dum-dum ammunition,
  The situation grows perplexed,
  The wicked country is annexed:
But, Oh! the change when o'er the wild,
Our sweet Humanity has smiled:
The savage shaves his shaggy locks,
Wears breaches and balbriggan socks,
Learns Euclid, classifies the fossils,
Draws pictures of the Twelve Apostles –
And now his pastor at the most
He is content to simply roast:
  Forgetful of the art of war,
  He smokes a twenty-cent cigar,
  He drinks not rum, his present care is
  For whisky and Apollinaris.
Content for this his land to change,
He fattens up and dies of mange.
  Lo! on the ashes of his Kraal,
  A Protestant Ca-the-der-al!

STEPHEN LEACOCK

Young Politician

What a lovely, lovely moon.
And it's in the constituency too.

ALAN JACKSON

Advertisement

Evangelical Vicar in want
of a portable, second-hand font,
  Would dispose, for the same,
  Of a portrait (in frame)
Of the Bishop, elect, of Vermont.

RONALD KNOX

Evil

Former angel, rebel devil,
What did Satan know of Evil?
All he knew was Guilt and Sin –
Words that make real Evil grin.

Red theatric hells may smoulder.
Evil's darker, older, colder.

CLARENCE DAY

The Use of Force

Do not believe
The use of force
Is how we change the social course;
The use of force
You surely know
Is how we keep the status quo.

JOHN K. ROOKE

Mr. Winston Churchill

Driven into devious channels by your longing outshine
All the deeds that gild the annals of a memorable line,
Ever planning new surprises public notice to engage,
In a dozen diff'rent guises have you bounded on the stage.

From your earliest days at Harrow, that renowned
      scholastic hive
Planted in your inmost marrow was the purpose to arrive;
Hence imperfectly enamoured of the groves of Academe,
For an ampler space you clamoured in the popular esteem.

Thus you made your life a solo in the high *bravura* style
Whether you were playing polo, or campaigning on the
      Nile;
Fraternising with a vulture, as you dodged the Burgher
      host,
Or entrancing with your culture readers of the *Morning
      Post*

Freed from regimental fetters which your soaring spirit
      galled,
By the magic spell of letters you were for a time
      enthralled
Chronicles of war inditing, touching the romantic lyre,
Or with filial fervour writing memoirs of your stormy
      sire.

Like the famed Pellæan stripling, whose unconscionable
      mind
Strove (in spite of Mr. Kipling) East and West in one to
      bind,
You, athirst for greater glories than one party could
      provide,
Were successively with Tories and with Radicals allied.

By ambition never sleeping spurred to startle and
    astound,
Yet your ear for ever keeping diligently to the ground,
By a premature conversation you neglected to discern
Chances for your self-assertion that may never more
    return.

As an orator effective in a strident florid strain,
Happiest in sheer invective, more thrasonic than humane;
Witty, yet too often sinning by your vitriolic verve;
Seldom you succeed in winning eulogy without reserve.

Modelling your style on Gibbon's (so the paragraphers
    say),
With your tropes and tags and ribbons you have made it
    wondrous gay;
Galvanising airs and graces old as the enternal hills,
Titivating commonplaces with sesquipedalian frills.

Quite the Admirable Crichton of an undistinguished age,
Like a Ministerial Triton 'mid the minnows you rampage;
With the frenzy of a Zulu plunging madly in the fray,
While the suave, impassive Lulu listens with serene
    dismay.

Now you hunt, a lively couple, with your little friend
    from Wales –
Both of you adroit and supple, on humanitarian trails;
Dear to all the cheapest papers for the copy you supply
Gratis by your agile capers cut to please the public eye.

Thus your course is splashed with colour, shot with
    Transatlantic vim,
And St. Stephen's would be duller if your sanguine star
    grew dim;
For although the Tories hate you, yet, when you are in the
    van,
Nobody should underrate you as a first-class fighting man.

CHARLES GRAVES

H

From Hitler's stone scrub Hitler's name,
But let the epitaph remain:
HERE LIES A MAN WHO HATED MEN
And underneath maintain:
WE WISH HIS MUM HAD FELT THE SAME.

CHRISTOPHER LOGUE

Drafts

They go to God knows where with songs of Blighty,
While I'm in bed with ribbons in my nightie.

NORA BOMFORD

The Pacifist

Pale Ebenezer thought it wrong to fight,
But Roaring Bill who killed him thought it right.

HILAIRE BELLOC

Pots

from: The Admiralty (Stores) List

Pots, Chamber, plain.
Pots, Chamber, with Admiralty monogram in blue,
    for hospital use.
Pots, Chamber, fluted, with Royal cypher in gold,
    for Flag officers only.
Pots, Chamber, round, rubber, lunatics.

ANONYMOUS

Lines on the Unmasking of the Surveyor of the Queen's Pictures

In 1979 it was revealed that Sir Anthony Blunt, an art historian, and a court official, had been spying for the Russians for over thirty-five years.

Poor old Bluntie! So they got him,
   'Mole Revealed' they say 'at last'.
On a bleak November morning,
   What an echo from the past!

Old Marlburian, I recall him,
   In his flannel bags and hat
Wandering by the River Talbot,
   Sometimes straining at a gnat.

Who'd have guessed it – 'Blunt a traitor'
   And an homosexualist?
Carrying on with Tar and waiter –
   There's a sight I'm glad I missed.

Now the nine day wonder's over,
   Back he goes to Maida Vale.
In his comfy little Rover.
   Home to gin and ginger ale.

Was it worth it? Does it matter?
   In the end we do not know.
Now I'm madder than a hatter,
   Goodness me! It's time to go.

RICHARD INGRAMS IN THE MANNER OF
SIR JOHN BETJEMAN

Russia

These bodies of men that here in glory lie
Once carried life about, but cause to live
Had little, lived on little, and to give,
Beyond their lives, had nothing. Cause to die
They had in plenty, cause to die for, none,
Excepting Freedom, a pretended one.

HEATHCOTE GARROD

U.S.A. 1492 – 1783

By dams that beavers engineered
By trails the French and Spanish cleared,
We sturdy Anglo-Saxons potted
The first inhabitants, and squatted.

KEITH PRESTON

We Zealots

We Zealots made up of stiff clay,
  The sour-looking children of sorrow,
While not over jolly to-day
  Resolve not to be wretched to-morrow.

We can't for a certainty tell
  What mirth may molest us on Monday
But, at least, to begin the week well,
  Let us all be unhappy on Sunday.

CHARLES, LORD NEAVES

The Nun

She was a very pretty Nun
Sad, delicate, and five feet one.

WINTHROP MACKWORTH PRAED

On Spies

Spies, you are Lights of State, but of base stuff,
Who, when you've burnt yourselves down to the snuff,
Stink, and are thrown away. Fair end enough.

BEN JONSON

Trinity

Upon my honour, I saw a Madonna
Hanging within a niche
Above the door of the private whore
Of the world's worst son of a bitch.

DOROTHY PARKER

A Whimsical Prophecy

When Tewkesbury mustard shall travel abroad,
And die in a land without magpie or toad;
When the sauce of the veal, joining three to a lion,
Shall devour a fifth, as the porpoise Orion:
Then lilies shall try to swim over the ferry
Where they shall be met with and drowned by a cherry;
While the children of France, with famine oppressed,
Will rejoice at a crust, as a knife at a feast.

BY A CERTAIN KNIGHT

73

Dooley is a Traitor

'So then you won't fight?'
'Yes, your Honour,' I said, 'that's right.'
'Now is it that you simply aren't willing,
Or have you a fundamental moral objection to killing?'
Says the judge, blowing his nose
And making his words stand to attention in long rows.
I stand to attention too, but with half a grin
(In my time I've done a good many in).
'No objection at all, sir,' I said.
'There's a deal of the world I'd rather see dead –
Such as Johnny Stubbs or Fred Settle or my last landlord,
    Mr Syme.
Give me a gun and your blessing, your Honour, and I'll be
    killing them all the time.
But my conscience says a clear no
To killing a crowd of gentleman I don't know.
Why, I'd as soon think of killing a worshipful judge,
High-court, like yourself (against whom, God knows,
    I've got no grudge –
So far), as murder a heap of foreign folk.
If you've got no grudge, you've got no joke
To laugh at after.'
                  Now the words never come flowing
Proper for me till I get the old pipe going.
And just as I was poking
Down baccy, the judge looks up sharp with 'No smoking,
Mr Dooley. We're not fighting this war for fun.
And we want a clearer reason why you refuse to carry a
    gun.
This war is not a personal feud, it's a fight
Against wrong ideas on behalf of the Right.
Mr Dooley, won't you help to destroy evil ideas?'
'Ah, your Honour, here's
The tragedy,' I said. 'I'm not a man of the mind.
I couldn't find it in my heart to be unkind
To an idea. I wouldn't know one if I saw one. I haven't
    one of my own.

So I'd best be leaving other people's alone.'
'Indeed,' he sneers at me, 'this defence is
Curious for someone with convictions in two senses.
A criminal invokes conscience to his aid
To support an individual withdrawal from a communal
    crusade
Sanctioned by God, led by the Church, against a godless,
    churchless nation!'
I asked his Honour for a translation.
'You talk of conscience,' he said. 'What do you know of
    the Christian creed?'
'Nothing, sir, except what I can read.
That's the most you can hope for from us jail-birds.
I just open the Book here and there and look at the words.
And I find when the Lord himself misliked an evil notion
He turned it into a pig and drove it squealing over a cliff
    into the ocean,
And the loony ran away
And lived to think another day.
There was a clean job done and no blood shed!
Everybody happy and forty wicked thoughts drowned
    dead.
A neat and Christian murder. None of your mad
    slaughter
Throwing away the brains with the blood and the baby
    with the bathwater.
Now I look at the war as a sportsman. It's a matter of
    choosing
The decentest way of losing.
Heads or tails, losers or winners,
We all lose, we're all damned sinners.
And I'd rather be with the poor cold people at the wall
    that's shot
Than the bloody guilty devils in the firing-line, in Hell
    and keeping hot.'
'But what right, Dooley, what right,' he cried,
'Have you to say the Lord is on your side?'
'That's a dirty crooked question,' back I roared.
'I said not the Lord was on my side, but I was on the side
    of the Lord.'

Then he was up at me and shouting,
But by and by he calms: 'Now we're not doubting
Your sincerity, Dooley, only your arguments,
Which don't make sense.'
('Hullo,' I thought, 'that's the wrong way round.
I may be skylarking a bit, but my brainpan's sound.')
Then biting his nail and sugaring his words sweet:
'Keep your head, Mr Dooley. Religion is clearly not up
    your street.
But let me ask you as a plain patriotic fellow
Whether you'd stand there so smug and yellow
If the foe were attacking your own dear sister.'
'I'd knock their brains out, mister,
On the floor,' I said. 'There,' he says kindly, 'I knew you
    were no pacifist.
It's your straight duty as a man to enlist.
The enemy is at the door.' You could have downed
Me with a feather. 'Where?' I gasp, looking round.
'Not this door,' he says angered. 'Don't play the clown.
But they're two thousand miles away planning to do us
    down.
Why, the news is full of the deeds of those murderers and
    rapers.'
'Your Eminence,' I said, 'my father told me never to
    believe the papers
But to go by my eyes,
And at two thousand miles the poor things can't tell truth
    from lies.'
His fearful spectacles glittered like the moon: 'For the last
    time what right
Has a man like you to refuse to fight?'
'More right,' I said, 'than you.
You've never murdered a man, so you don't know what it
    I won't do.
I've done it in good hot blood, so haven't I the right to
    make bold
To declare that I shan't do it in cold?'

Then the judge rises in a great rage
And writes DOOLEY IS A TRAITOR in black upon a
     page
And tells me I must die.
'What me?' says I.
'If you still won't fight.'
'Well, yes, your Honour,' I said, 'that's right.'

JAMES MICHIE

International Conference

To kill its enemies and cheat its friends,
Each nation its prerogative defends;
Yet some their efforts for goodwill maintain,
In hope, in faith, in patience, and in vain.

COLIN ELLIS

Arts & Entertainment

LvB

Higgledy-piggledy
Ludwig van Beethoven
Bored by requests for some
Music to hum,

Finally answered with
Oversimplicity,
'Here's my Fifth Symphony:
Duh, duh, duh, DUM!'

E. WILLIAM SEAMAN

The Call of the Eastern Quail

An Examination Question from *Whistling as an Art* by
Agnes Woodward, New York, 1923

What is the hewie chirp?
How written by note?
    What is triple-tonguing?
    The reverse chirp? How expressed?
What are the quittas?

Define the whit-char.
Define the e-chew.
What is the chut-ee?
How made? How expressed?

Define the ascending and descending yodels
    dipped yodels and quivers.
What are the two liquid bird figures?

What is the lup-ee?
What is the e-lup?
How made? How expressed?
What is the call of the Eastern Quail?
What is the call of the Western Quail?

With tongue and teeth whistlers
    what can be substituted for
    the yodel, lup, hedala and cudalee?

What is the wave?
On what pulsation do we stop?

FOUND BY GEORGE HITCHCOCK

The Failure

O why ain't I blessed wiv green fingers
Why ain't me plants strong an' tall
How come all me neighbours reap fruit from their
    labours
While I never reaps bugger-all?

Me beetroots is pale an' anaemic
Me leeks grow no thicker than threads
Me cues an' tomarters is chronic non-starters
Cos me seeds never rise from their beds.

Me parsnips is parst orl redemption
Me peaches an' pears never crop
Me broad-beans an' marrers ain't fit for the sparrers
An' I'm buyin' me spuds up the shop.

I've giv 'em orl kinds of pertection
I've tret 'em like fammerly pets
Yet me bushes an' trees is beset wiv diseases
Wot nobody else never gets.

I works an' I waits an' I worries
I never 'as time ter relax
Me fingers is bleedin' from forkin' an' weedin'
While uvvers lie flat on their backs.

Me knuckles is covered in plasters
Me neck 'as a pernamint crick
Me muscles is achin' from hoein' an' rakin'
An' me back ain't arf givin' me stick.

I've read every book in the lib'ry
Consulted the experts by post
I've tried orl the capers described in the papers
An' killed orf more plantlife than most.

But, I've never been known as a quitter
An' one day I'm gonna perfect
By intensive research down the "Angler an' Perch"
A garden wot thrives on neglect.

J. J. WEBSTER

On Scott Fitzgerald

We've found this Scott Fitzgerald chap
  A chipper charming child;
He's taught us how the flappers flap,
And why the whipper-snappers snap,
  What makes the women wild.
But now he should make haste to trap
  The ducats in his dipper.
The birds that put him on the map
Will shortly all begin to rap
  And flop to something flipper.

KEITH PRESTON

The Changing Face
of an Actress

After curtain calls
Her
       face
            falls
– Then someone says Darling
You were marvellous
– and she picks it up again!

MICHAEL HOROVITZ

Original

Saith one : 'To no school I belong;
No living Master leads me wrong;
Nor do I, for the things I know,
A debt to any dead man owe' –
Which means, in phrasing less polite :
'I am a Fool in my own Right.'

JOHANN WOLFGANG VON GOETHE
TRANSLATED BY AUSTIN DOBSON

On His Violet

Serene is the morning, the lark leaves his nest,
   And signs a salute to the dawn.
The sun with his splendour illumines the East,
   And brightens the dew on the lawn.
Whilst the sons of debauch to indulgence give way,
   And slumber the prime of their hours,
Let us, my dear Stella, the garden survey,
   And make our remarks on the flowers.

The gay gaudy tulip observe as you walk,
   How flaunting the gloss of its vest!
How proud! and how stately it stands on its stalk,
   In beauty's diversity dressed!
From the rose, the carnation, the pink and the clove,
   What odours delightfully spring!
The South wafts a richer perfume to the grove,
   As he brushes the leaves with his wing.

Apart from the rest, in her purple array,
   The violet humbly retreats;
In modest concealment she peeps on the day,
   Yet none can excel her in sweets:
So humble that, though with unparalled grace
   She might e'en palace adorn,
She oft in the hedge hides her innocent face,
   And grows at the foot of the thorn.

WILLIAM WOTY

A Song by a Poet against Music

Musicks's a Crotchet the Sober think Vain;
   The Fiddle's a Wooden Projection;
Tunes are but flirts of a Whimsical Brain,
   Which the Bottle brings best to Perfection.
Musicians are Half-Witted, Merry, and Mad;
   The same are all those that Admire 'em;
They're Fools if they play, unless they'er well Paid;
   And the others are Block-heads to Hire-'em.

        Chorus
        The Organ's but Humming,
        Theorbo but Thrumming,
        The Viol and Voice
        Is but Jingle and Noise
        The Bagpipe and Fiddle
        Goes Twedle and Diddle,
        The Hoitboy and Flute
        Is but Toot a Toot Toot.

NED WARD

84

A Song by a Musician against Poetry

Poetry's Fabulous, Loose, and Prophane;
   For Trust you must never depend on't;
'Tis the Juvenal Froth of a Frenzical Brain,
   Hung with Jingling Tags at the end-on't.
Poets are Poor, full of Whimsie and Flight,
   For Amorous Fops to delight-in;
They're Fools if they write, lest they got Money by't,
   And they're Blockheads that pay 'em for writing.

         Chorus
        Their soft Panegyric,
        Is Praise beyond Merit;
        Their Lampoon and Satyr,
        Is Spight and Ill-Nature;
        Their Plays and Romances,
        Are Fables and Fancies;
        Their Drolls and their Farces,
        Are bald as our Arses.

NED WARD

The Tutor

A Tutor who tooted the flute,
Tried to teach two young tooters to toot;
    Said the two to the tutor,
     'Is it harder to toot or
To tutor two tooters to toot?'

CAROLYN WELLS

Bon Mot

When Whistler's strongest colors fade,
    When inks and canvas rot,
Those jokes on Oscar Wilde he made
    Will dog him unforgot.

For gags still set the world agog
    When fame begins to flag,
And, like the tail that wagged the dog,
    The smart tale dogs the wag.

KEITH PRESTON

The Amateurs

Our deportment is graceful but frigid;
   We smile, but we seldom applaud:
When late comers push by we observe with a sigh
   That 'they order things better abroad.'

We have dined very simply and early,
   For only by habits austere
Can we hope to attain to a critical vein
   And a judgment impartial and clear.

In the intervals, liquid refreshment
   We leave to the vicious and weak:
More refreshing to us is to sit and discuss
   The defects of the actors' technique.

When the curtain goes down amid 'bravos,'
   We murmur a word of dispraise.
Then we proudly file out, having proved beyond doubt
   That we really appreciate plays.

Let us hope, for the sale of the drama,
   When next we endeavour to act
That our friends who are there will be equally fair,
   And behave with commensurate tact.

COLIN ELLIS

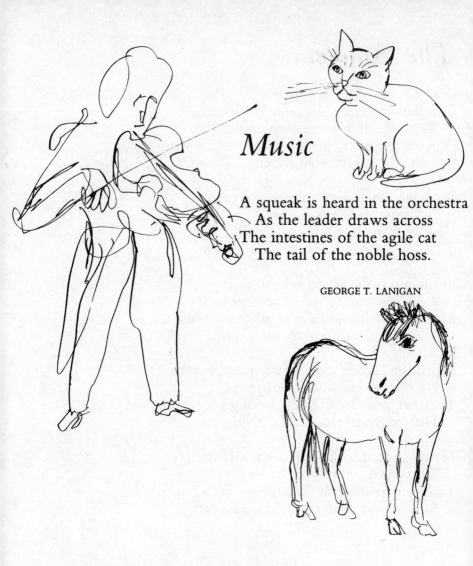

Music

A squeak is heard in the orchestra
As the leader draws across
The intestines of the agile cat
The tail of the noble hoss.

GEORGE T. LANIGAN

The Music Critic

Mr Ernest Newman
Said: Next week Schumann
But when next week came
It was Wagner just the same.

ANONYMOUS

The Power of Art

It was a chill November eve and on the busy town
A heavy cloud of yellow fog was sinking slowly down;
Upon the bridge of Waterloo, a prey to mad despair,
There stood a man with heavy brow, and deep-lined face
    of care.

One ling'ring look around he gave, he on the river cast
That sullen stare of rash resolve he meant should be his
    last.
Far down the old cathedral rose, a shadow grey and dim,
The light of day would dawn on that but ne'er again on
    him.

One plunge within the murky stream would end the bitter
    strife
'What rests there now,' he sobbed aloud, 'to bid me cling
    to life?'
Just then the sound of stamping feet smote on his
    list'ning ear,
A sandwich-man upon his beat paused 'neath the
    lamplight clear.

One hurried glance – he read the board that hung upon his
    back,
He leapt down from the parapet, and smote his thigh a
    smack.
'I must see that,' he cried – the words that put his woe to
    flight
Were 'John S. Clark as Acres at the Charing Cross
    tonight.'

ANONYMOUS

Search for Grace

More and
more boiling fowls are
taking
ballet lessons.

Estimated numbers:
1975 – one.
1976 – none.
1977 – none.
1980 – one.
1985 – one.
1987 – two.
1993 – one.

IVOR CUTLER

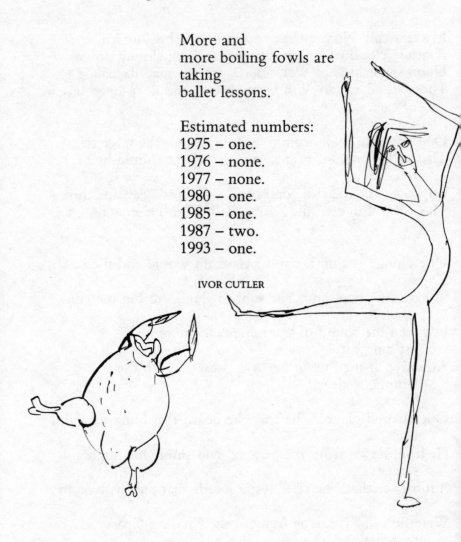

On Shakespeare

Master Will, so cussed human,
Careless clouted God of speech,
Is their twist of man or woman
Too well hidden for thy reach?

EZRA POUND

Mozart

Mozart
Could never resist a tart.
In the ordinary way
He ate seven or eight a day.

E. J. EVANS

Abroad

O for a Shakespear's pencil, while I trace
In Nature's breathing paint, the dreary waste
Of Buxton...

WILLIAM WHITEHEAD

The Villa by the Sea

Mine is that delightful villa,
　　Sweetly nesting by the sea;
Yet I sigh for a scintilla
　　Of the bliss it promised me.

Though a pleasant cottage orné,
　　Rich in trellis-work and flowers,
Here to sit and end my journey,
　　How could I beguile the hours?

Love of Nature is a duty,
　　And I fain would love it more.
But I weary of the beauty.
　　I have seen for weeks before.

Lofty are the hills and regal,
　　Still they are the hills of old;
And like any other sea-gull
　　Is the sea-gull I behold.

Tiresome 'tis to be a dreamer.
　　When will it be time to dine?
Oh, that almost stand-still steamer,
How it crawls across the brine!

JAMES HEDDERWICK

The Bloody Orkneys

This bloody town's a bloody cuss –
No bloody trains, no bloody bus,
And no one cares for bloody us –
    In bloody Orkney.

The bloody roads are bloody bad,
The bloody folks are bloody mad,
They'd make the brightest bloody sad,
    In bloody Orkney.

All bloody clouds, and bloody rains,
No bloody kerbs, no bloody drains,
The Council's got no bloody brains,
    In bloody Orkney.

Everything's so bloody dear,
A bloody bob, for bloody beer,
And is it good? – no bloody fear,
    In bloody Orkney.

The bloody "flicks" are bloody old,
The bloody seats are bloody cold,
You can't get in for bloody gold
    In bloody Orkney.

The bloody dances make you smile,
The bloody band is bloody vile,
It only cramps your bloody style,
    In bloody Orkney.

No bloody sport, no bloody games,
No bloody fun, the bloody dames
Won't even give their bloody names
    In bloody Orkney.

Best bloody place is bloody bed,
With bloody ice on bloody head,
You might as well be bloody dead,
    In bloody Orkney.

CAPTAIN HAMISH BLAIR

Natura in Urbe

I like my trees complete with railings,
    I like my grass encompassed by
Park fences. And my other failings
    Include a preference for sky
Well steeple-chased and tower-dissected,
    Through rural friends adjudge it droll,
If not inscrutably affected,
    To stay in town to till the soul.

MARGARET FISHBACK

The Patriot – A Very Indian Poem in Indian English

I am standing for peace and non-violence.
Why world is fighting, fighting,
Why all people of world
Are not following Mahatma Gandhi,
I am simply not understanding,
Ancient Indian Wisdom is 100% correct.
I should say even 200% correct.
But modern generation is neglecting –
To much going for fashion and foreign thing.

Other day I am reading in newspaper
(Every day I'm reading Times of India
To improve my English language)
How one goonda fellow
Throw stone at Indirabehn.
Must be student unrest fellow, I am thinking.
Friends, Romans, countrymen, I am saying
(To myself)
Lend me the ears.
Everything is coming –
Regeneration, Remuneration, Contraception.
Be patiently, brothers and sisters.

You want one glass *lassi*?
Very good for digestion.
With little salt lovely drink,
Better than wine,
Not that I am ever tasting wine.
I'm the total teetotaler, completely total.
But I say
Wine is for the drunkards only.

What you think of prospect of world peace?
Pakistan behaving like this,
China behaving like that.
It is making me very sad I am telling you.
Really, most harassing me.
All men are brothers, no?
In India also
Gujaraties, Maharashtrians, Hindiwallahs
All brothers
Though some are having funny habits.
Still, you tolerate me,
I tolerate you,
One day Ram Rajya is surely coming.

You are going?
But you will visit again
Any time, any day,
I am not believing in ceremony.
Always I am enjoying your company.

NISSIM EZEKIEL

The Despair of My Muse

Ye great brown hares; grown madder through the Spring!
  Ye birds that utilise your tiny throttles
To make the archways of the forest ring
Or go about your easy house-hunting!
  Ye toads! ye axolotls!

Ye happy blighters all, that squeal and squat
  And fly and browse where'er the mood entices,
Noting in every hedge or woodland grot
The swelling surge of sap, but noting not
  The rise in current prices!

Could I but share your diet cheap and rude,
  Your simple ways in trees and copses lurking;
But no, I need a pipe and lots of food,
A comfortable chair on which to brood –
  Silence! the bard is working.

Could I but know that freedom from all care
  That comes, I say, from gratis sets of suitings
And homes that need not premium nor repair
Except with sticks and mud and moss and hair,
  My! there would be some flutings.

And often as I heard the throstles vamp,
  Pouring their liquid notes like golden syrup,
Out would I go and round the garden tramp,
Wearing goloshes if the day were damp,
  And imitate their chirrup.

Or, bowling peacefully upon my bike,
  Well breakfasted, by no distractions flustered,
Pause near a leafy copse or brambled dyke,
And answer song for song the black-backed shrike,
  The curlew and the bustard.

Lambs, buds, leap up; the lark to heaven climbs;
  Bread does the same; the price of baccy's brutal;
And save (I do not note it in The Times)
They make exceptions for evolving rhymes,
  Dashed if I mean to tootle!

                    E.V. KNOX

The Trip

All the way
To L.A.
And back.
Hack.

MICHAEL HASTINGS

To a Friend in Search of Rural Seclusion

When all else fails,
try Wales.

CHRISTOPHER LOGUE

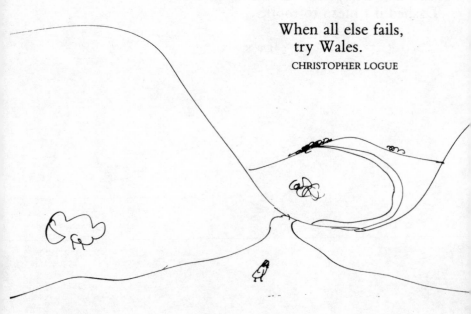

On Lido's Shore

On Lido's shore
  And Bailey's Beach
Beasts used to roar
  Or weirdly screech.
With hearty passion
  They would sport,
Where wealth and fashion
  Now resort.

In silken state
  Girls stroll, entranced,
Today, where great
  Behemoth danced.
Around them, hosts
  Of bathers gone,
Whose giant ghosts
  Still linger on.

CLARENCE DAY

Upon my New built House At Easton, near Norwich.

Not vex'd by children, and unawed by spouse,
To freedom Buxton builds her humble house;
A calm retreat which pining envy flies,
And vile detraction with 10,000 lies!
Here free to live by Nature's wholesome rules,
No slave to fashion or to fashion's fools.
To friendship open, and its sober joys,
Spinstress, no more lament, thus,
                    Fix your choice.

MRS SARAH BUXTON

Upon the Same

In frantick fury and in wild despair,
Neglected Buxton rears her mansion here;
From a gay world, from beaux and balls she flies,
And Bath and Tunbridge leaves to brighter eyes;
Tir'd of herself, and tiring all mankind,
Her raving restless soul this cell designed,
Choak'd up with pride ill nature and ill blood,
And fix'd her BEDLAM in the little Wood.

R. GARDNER

102

A Country Summer Pastoral

I would flee from the city's rule and law,
　　From its fashion and form cut loose,
And go where the strawberry grows on its straw,
　　And the gooseberry on its goose;
Where the catnip tree is climbed by the cat
　　As she crouches for her prey –
The guileless and unsuspecting rat
　　On the rattan bush at play.

I will watch at ease for the saffron cow
　　And the cowlet in their glee
As they leap in joy from bough to bough
　　On the top of the cowslip tree;
Where the musical partridge drums on his drum.
　　And the woodchuck chucks his wood,
And the dog devours the dogwood plum
　　In the primitive solitude.

And then to the whitewashed dairy I'll turn,
　　Where the dairymaid hastening hies,
Her ruddy and golden-haired butter to churn,
　　From the milk of the butterflies;
And I'll rise at morn with the early bird,
　　To the fragrant farmyard pass
When the farmer turns his beautiful herd
　　Of grasshoppers out to grass.

ANONYMOUS

Business

Bankers

Most bankers dwell in marble halls,
Which they get to dwell in because they encourage
    deposits and discourage withdralls.

OGDEN NASH

Meaning Business

Charge your glasses, be upstanding,
Toast the saints whose one concern
Is to see that current prices
Coincide with what you earn.

Industry is such a neat word,
Shrewdly culled from Roget's lists,
No one hopefully will notice
That they mean industrialists.

Patriotic, conscience-stricken,
Choking on the food they eat,
They present a noble image
To the victim in the street.

Pensioners, the weak and spastic,
Gaunt in rat-infested holes,
Robbed from birth of health and reason,
Trouble their immortal souls.

They are pledged to honest trading,
Hardly ever to defraud,
While their boundless love of country,
Prompts them to invest abroad.

Leave them to the job they're bred for,
Give these heroes half a chance,
And you'll see the Venus fly-trap
Flourishing among their plants.

RODGER WOODIS

Advice to Copywriters

When your client's hopping mad
Put his picture in the ad.
If he still should prove refractory
Add a picture of his factory.

ANONYMOUS

On those who Deal in, or Who Exhibit, Manuscripts

Accurst, who brings to light of day
The writing I have cast away.
But blest be he who shows them not
And lets the kind word take the lot.

W. B. YEATS

Meetings

Implement, finalise, thrust and imbue,
Interface, maximise, meet and review.
Orchestrate, optimise, cost and compute.
Dialogue, quantitise, rate and refute.

HARRY BOYLE

City Proverb

Sell in May
And go away.

ANONYMOUS

Now We Are Sick

Christopher
        Robin
             goes
                  hippety
                      hoppety
immigrants
        bring down
                the value of
                      property

ADRIAN MITCHELL

Scientists
& Doctors

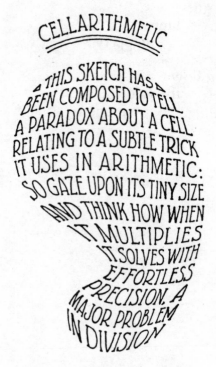

CELLARITHMETIC

THIS SKETCH HAS BEEN COMPOSED TO TELL A PARADOX ABOUT A CELL RELATING TO A SUBTLE TRICK IT USES IN ARITHMETIC: SO GAZE UPON ITS TINY SIZE AND THINK HOW WHEN IT MULTIPLIES IT SOLVES WITH EFFORTLESS PRECISION, A MAJOR PROBLEM IN DIVISION

GERALD LYNTON KAUFMAN

Method

O Cuckoo! shall I call thee Bird
Or but a wandering Voice?
State the alternative preferred
With reasons for your choice.

J. BRONOWSKI

Progress

Higgledy-piggledy
Thomas A. Edison
Turned on a switch with a
Wave of his wand.

Giving his name to some
Organizational
Chaps in whose light we are
Now being conned.

SALLY BELFRAGE

Ape into Man

A scientist evolved a plan
To turn an ape into a man,
But by the time that he had done
The ape was nearly seventy-one.
So all attempts to educate
The weary beast were rather late.

The ape, however, didn't mind.
He didn't wish to be refined.

CLARENCE DAY

111

To Madame X with a Brace of Duck

I've dispatch'd, my dear madam, this scrap of a letter,
To say that Miss —— is very much better.
A Regular Doctor no longer she lacks.
And therefore I've sent her a couple of Quacks.

DR. EDWARD JENNER

Lines

Composed after learning that the plan to raise a statue of him had been scotched.

England's ingratitude still blots
The scutcheon of the brave and free;
I saved you from a million spots.
And now you grudge a spot to me.

DR EDWARD JENNER

The Doctor

The doctor lives by chicken pox
    by measles, and by mumps.
He keeps a microbe in a box
    and cheers him when he jumps

at unsuspecting children, who
    have two important nurses;
but if it bounds where less than two
    are kept, he simply curses.

His greed is such that though you ache
    in every limb, be sure
if there is nothing else to take,
    he'll take your temperature.

And if at first he can't succeed,
    he has another try,
and takes your pulse. Some people plead
    'The man must live!' But why?

HUMBERT WOLFE

Yet What Are All Such Gaities to Me

Yet what are all such gaities to me
Whose life is full of indices and surds?

$$x^2 + 7x + 53$$
$$= 11/3$$

LEWIS CARROLL

114

The Purple Yeti

How can the purple yeti be so red,
Or chestnuts, like a widgeon, calmly groan?
No sheep is quite as crooked as a bed,
Though chickens ever try to hide a bone.
I grieve that greasy turnips slowly march:
Indeed, inflated is the icy pig:
For as the alligator strikes the larch,
So sighs the grazing goldfish for a wig.
Oh, has the pilchard argued with a top?
Say never that the parsnip is too weird!
I tell thee that a wolf-man will not hop
And no man ever praised the convex beard.
Effulgent is the day when bishops turn:
So let not then the doctor wake the urn!

JONATHAN R. PARTINGTON AND A COMPUTER

Philosophy

Women have their faults,
Men have only two:
Everything they say,
Everything they do.

ANONYMOUS

Proverbial Ballade

Fine words won't turn the icing pink;
A wild rose has no employees;
Who boils his socks will make them shrink;
Who catches cold is sure to sneeze.
Who has two legs must wash two knees;
Who breaks the egg will find the yolk;
Who locks his door will need his keys –
So say I and so say the folk.

You can't shave with a tiddlywink,
Nor make red wine from garden peas,
Nor show a blindworm how to blink,
Nor teach an old racoon Chinese.
The juiciest orange feels the squeeze;
Who spends his portion will be broke;
Who has no milk can make no cheese –
So say I and so say the folk.

He makes no blot who has no ink,
Nor gathers honey who keeps no bees.
The ship that does not float will sink;
Who'd travel far must cross the seas.
Lone wolves are seldom seen in threes;
A conker ne'er becomes an oak;
Rome wasn't built by chimpanzees –
So say I and so say the folk.

Envoi

Dear friends! If adages like these
Should seem banal, or just a joke,
Remember fish don't grow on trees –
So say I and so say the folk.

WENDY COPE

117

For Mr William Martin

The Northumberland Poet and Philosopher, who, through the contemptible and disgusting egotism with which his works abound, reveals the following beliefs: that he was sent by the Providence of God into this World for the purpose of Enlightening it, that Air is the Cause of all Things, that Mrs Bebe Trumbull's smoke-jack is a form of Perpetual Motion, and that Sir Humphry Davy ought to be tried for the man-slaughter, if not the murder of those who have been killed in the Mines where his Lamp has been used.

Friend Martin, pray cease to Lecture pro bono,
And spew out no more of thy Lore.
Cans't thou make men wiser? – O, no no, O, no no,
O Martin pray Lecture no more.

Friend Martin, abandon thy hope to gain Fame,
Thou maggoty, goggle-eyed, bore.
Both the quick and the dead cry, O, no no, O, no no,
O Philosopher, Lecture no more.

Friend Martin, abjure to Lecture for pence;
Thy wife will continue to whore.
Dame Nature cries, no no, O no no, O no no,
O Poet, pray Lecture no more.

G. W. COUPER

On the Death of a German Philosopher

He wrote The I and the It
He wrote The It and the Me
He died at Marienbad
And now we are all at sea.

STEVIE SMITH

Xantippe said to Socrates:
You're drunk, just look at you.
He said: one must doubt what one sees
Nothing is wholly true.
He ranks as a philosopher
She as the classic shrew.

BERTOLT BRECHT, TRANSLATED BY JOHN WILLETT

A Meditation

There is a window in my soul
  Which opens on the world of art,
Circumference as well as goal
  Of Spirit and its counterpart.

I watch the urgent strife of form,
  Where vistas of a realm unmade
Impinge on the essential norm
  Wherewith posterities have played.

The intuitions of an age
  Too sibilant to be out-won,
Too care-free to redeem the rage
  Of services that shrink the sun,

Are windowed in the Absolute
  And over-leap the spume of things,
Unjettisoned upon the mute
  Curtailment of the poet's wings.

SANDYS WASON

The Pessimist

Nothing to do but work,
  Nothing to eat but food,
Nothing to wear but clothes,
  To keep one from going nude.

Nothing to breathe but air,
  Quick as a flash 'tis gone;
Nowhere to fall but off,
  Nowhere to stand but on.

Nothing to comb but hair,
  Nowhere to sleep but in bed,
Nothing to weep but tears,
  Nothing to bury but dead.

Nothing to sing but songs,
  Ah, well, alas! alack!
Nowhere to go but out,
  Nowhere to come but back.

Nothing to see but sights,
  Nothing to quench but thirst.
Nothing to have but what we've got.
  Thus thro' life we are cursed.

BENJAMIN FRANKLIN KING

The Wishes of an Elderly Man

I wish I loved the Human Race:
I wish I loved its silly face;
I wish I liked the way it walks;
I wish I liked the way it talks;
And when I'm introduced to one
I wish I thought, What Jolly Fun!

WALTER RALEIGH

Epitaph on a Prig

Here lies a man who always thought
That he was acting as he ought.
He turned his cheek to every blow
And never said 'I told you so,'
Nor claimed with any outward spite
The mean revenge of being right.
He died at three score years and ten
Detested by his fellow men
But conscious of a Heavenly Crown –
'Go down!' St. Peter said 'Go down!'

COLIN ELLIS

Vice and Virtue

If Vice were punished and Virtue paid,
    As I thought when I was young,
The world would be better – but I'm afraid,
    That I should have soon been hung.

If men were valiant and true to trust,
    As once I used to think,
Then I should have died from a bayonet thrust,
    Or ever I'd learned to drink.

If Cupid carried the fatal darts,
    That once I thought he bore,
We all should perish of broken hearts
    By the time we were twenty-four.

We cannot be merry and wise and good,
    As I hoped when I was a lad,
So I have endeavoured as best I could,
    To be merry and wise and bad.

COLIN ELLIS

Poets

This poet, in a lifetime all too short O,
Died both in duodecimo and quarto;
Recent attempts his twice-dead life to save O
Enabled him to die in Crown octavo.

PONCE-DENIS ECOUCHARD LEBRUN TRANSLATED BY
GEORGE   ROSTREVOR HAMILTON

Oberflächenübersetzung

A surface translation of William Wordsworth's 'My
Heart Leaps Up When I Behold'

mai hart lieb zapfen eibe hold
er renn bohr in sees kai
so was sieht wenn mai läuft begehen
so es sieht nahe emma mähen
so biet wenn ärschel grollt
ohr leck met ei!
seht steil dies fader rosse mähen
in teig kurt wisch mai desto bier
baum deutsche deutsch bajonett schur alp eiertier

my heart leaps up when I behold
a rainbow in the sky
so was it when my life began
so is it now I am a man
so be it when I shall grow old
or let me die!
the child is father of the man
and I could wish my days to be
bound each to each by natural piety

ERNST JANDL AND WILLIAM WORDSWORTH

The Moron

See the happy moron,
  He doesn't give a damn.
I wish I were a moron;
  My God! perhaps I am!

ANONYMOUS

Byron and Drury

Byron lay, lazily lay,
Hid from lesson and game away,
Dreaming poetry, all alone,
Up-a-top of the Peachey stone.
All in a fury enters Drury,
  Sets him grammar and Virgil due;
Poets shouldn't have, shouldn't have, shouldn't have,
  Poets shouldn't have work to do.

EDWARD ERNEST BOWEN

Lines

Written on paper and pinned to the gate of a
neglected field near Bateman's, Sussex, early in this
century. They were remembered by Mr Donald Burgess
of Dallington, Sussex, and taken down from him by
Mrs Clare Lyon of Dallington.

This field with thistles doth abound
And no one comes to mow it.
To whom d'you think this field belongs?
Mr Kipling the poet.

The Session of the Poets

At the Session of Poets, held lately in London,
  The Bard of Freshwater was voted the chair:
With his tresses unbrush'd, and his shirt-collar undone,
  He loll'd at his ease like a good-humour'd bear;
'Come, boys!' he exclaimed, 'we'll be merry together!'
  And lit up his pipe with a smile on his cheek;
While with eye, like a skipper's, cock'd up at the
                                    weather,
  Sat the Vice-Chairman Browning, thinking in Greek.

Right stately sat Arnold, his black gown adjusted
  Genteelly, his Rhine wine deliciously iced,
With puddingish England serenely disgusted,
  And looking in vain (in the mirror) for 'Geist';
He heark'd to the Chairman, with 'Surely!' and 'Really?'
  Aghast at both collar and cutty of clay,
Then felt in his pocket, and breath'd again freely.
  On touching the leaves of his own classic play.

Close at hand lingered Lytton, whose Icarus winglets
  Had often betrayed him in regions of rhyme;
How glittered the eye underneath his grey ringlets,
  A hunger within it unlessen'd by time!
Remoter sat Bailey – satirical, surly –
  Who studied the language of Goethe too soon,
And sang himself hoarse to the stars very early,
  And crack'd a weak voice with too lofty a tune.

What was said? what was done? was there prosing or
                                          rhyming?
   Was nothing noteworthy in deed or in word?
Why, just as the hour of supper was chiming,
   The only event of the evening occurred.
Up jumped, with his neck stretching out like a gander,
   Master Swinburne, and squeal'd, glaring out thro' his
                                          hair,
'All virtue is bosh! Hallelujah for Landor!
   I disbelieve wholly in everything! There!'

With language so awful he dared then to treat 'em
   Miss Ingelow fainted in Tennyson's arms,
Poor Arnold rush'd out, crying 'Soccl' inficetum!'
   And great bards and small bards were full of alarms.
Till Tennyson, flaming and red as a gipsy,
   Struck his fist on the table and utter'd a shout;
'To the door with the boy! Call a cab! He is tipsy!'
   And they carried the naughty young gentleman out.

ROBERT BUCHANAN

Milton

Milton, my help, my prop, my stay,
My well of English undefiled,
It struck me suddenly today
You must have been *an awful* child.

MAX BEERBOHM

The Highland Poet

On Perth's bleak hills I chanced to spy
An aged poet six feet high,
With brittled hair and visage blighted,
Wall-eyed, bare-arsed, and second-sighted.

THOMAS TICKELL

Byron

Oh, thou immortal bard!
Men may condemn the song
   That issued from thy heart sublime,
Yet alas! its music sweet
Has left an echo that will sound
   Thro' the lone corridors of Time.

Thou immortal Byron!
Thy inspired genius
   Let no man attempt to smother –
May all that was good within thee
Be attributed to Heaven,
   All that was evil – to thy mother.

J. GORDON COOGLER

131

For Laughing At A Stranger Who Broke Wind

He he he he he
he he he he he he he
he he he he he
he he he he he he he
he he he he he he he.

KABOCHA GENNARI

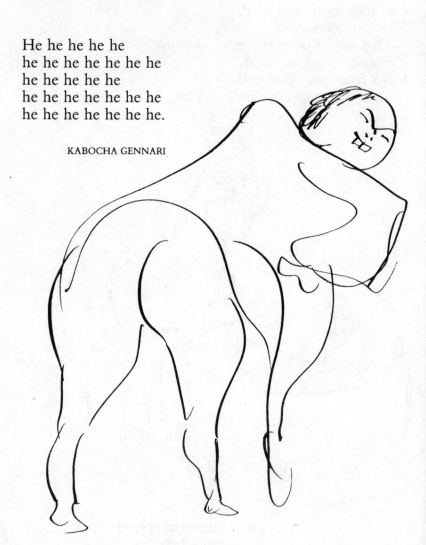

HE, in Japanese, means fart.

Heine

There may be nothing finer
Than the poetry of Heine,
But the news that Mr Upton Sinclair, Sir Rabindranath
  Tagore, and Mr John Galsworthy are on a committee
  formed to discuss the erection of a memorial on his
  behalf
Makes me laugh.

J. B. MORTON

WSL and EP

Walter Savage Landor
Never used and/or.
In Ezra Pound
and/ors abound.

M.C./C.L.

Relations

Charley Lamb, while yet a child,
    In a churchyard, on a day,
Walking with his sister mild,
    Spelling o'er the grave-stones gray,
Seeing nought but praise, where'er
    An inscription met his eye,
Wondering, ask'd her, 'Mary, where
    Do the wicked people lie?'

HENRY SAMBROKE LEIGH

Aunty Jane, Aunty Vi, and Uncle Jake

When Aunty Jane
Became a Crane
She put one leg behind her head;
And even when the clock struck ten
Refused to go to bed.

When Aunty Vi
Became a Fly
Her favourite nephew
Sought her life;
How could he know
That with each blow
He bruised his Uncle's wife?

When Uncle Jake
Became a Snake
He never found it out;
And so as no one mentions it
One sees him still about.

MERVYN PEAKE

Misplaced Sympathy

Little Benny sat one evening,
  Looking o'er his picture-book:
Suddenly his mother noticed
  On his face a troubled look.

He was gazing on a picture, –
  'Christians in the early days,'
When the cruel tyrant Nero
  Harassed them in various ways.

'Twas a family of Christians,
  Torn by lions fierce and wild,
In the horrible arena,
  Which had thus distressed the child.

Thinking it a golden moment
  To impress his youthful mind
With our freedom, dearly purchased,
  And by martyrs' blood refined,

His good mother told the story
  Of their persecutions sore,
While he listened, all attention,
  And the picture pondered o'er.

See, my child, those hungry lions,
    How upon the group they fall!
'Tis a sight, my precious darling.
    That the bravest might appal.

Then, with little lip a-quiver,
    "Mamma, look!" says little Benny:
"Little lion in the corner,
    Mamma, isn't gettin' any!"

CHARLES FOLLEN ADAMS

Aunt Jane

'Mamma' said Amanda 'I want to know what
  Our relatives mean when they say
That Aunt Jane is a Gorgon who ought to be shot,
  Or at any rate taken away.

'Pray what is a Gorgon and why do you shoot
  It? Or are its advances refused?
Or is it perhaps a maleficent Brute?
  I protest I am wholly bemused.

'The Term,' said her Mother, 'is certain to pain,
  And is quite inexcusably rude.
Moreover Aunt Jane, though uncommonly plain,
  Is also uncommonly good.

'She provides information without hesitation.
  For people unwilling to learn
And often bestows good advice upon those
  Who give her no thanks in return.

'She is down before anyone's up in the place –
  That is, up before anyone's down.
Her Domestics are awed by the shape of her face
  And they tremble with fear at her frown.

'Her visiting list is of Clergymen who
  Have reached a respectable age,
And she pays her companion Miss Angela Drew
  A sufficient and regular wage.

'Her fortune is large, though we often remark
  On a modesty rare in the rich;
For her nearest and dearest are quite in the dark
  As to what she will leave, or to which.

'Her conduct has ever been totally free
   From censorious whispers of ill,
At any rate, since 1903 –
   And probably earlier still.

'Your Father's dear sister presents, in a word,
   A model for all of her sex,
With a firmness of will that is never deterred,
   And a confidence nothing can vex.

'I can only desire that you too should aspire
   To such earthly reward as appears
In a high reputation, at present entire,
   After Heaven knows how many years.

'So in future remember to turn a deaf ear
   To detraction – and now run away
To your brothers and sisters whose laughter I hear
   In the garden below us at play.'

'Oh thank you, Mamma!' said Amanda at that,
   And ran off to the innocent band
Who were merrily burying Thomas the Cat
   Right up to his neck in the sand.

HILAIRE BELLOC

Grandpapa

Here is a portrait. Here one can
Descry those purely human features
Whereby, since first the world began,
Man has with ease distinguished man
From humbler fellow-creatures
And seldom, whatso'er his shape
Mistaken him for dog or ape.

Inspect this subject well, and note
The whiskers centrally divided,
The silken stock about the throat,
The loose but elegant frock-coat,
The boots (elastic-sided)
And you'll at once remark: "Ah, ha!
This must, of course, be Grandpapa!"

'Tis he, of feudal types the last,
By all his peers revered, respected;
His lines in pleasant places cast
Where churls saluted as he pass'd
And maidens genuflected,
And, if he chanced to meet the vicar,
The latter's pulse would beat the quicker.

In politics it was his rule
To be broadminded but despotic:
In argument he kept quite cool
Knowing a man to be a fool
And most unpatriotic
Who differed from the views that he
Had cherished from the age of three.

Once, I recall – a sad affair –
When as a child of years still tender,
I chanced to sit in his armchair,
He seized me roughly by the hair
And flung me in the fender.
He had such quaint impulsive ways;
I didn't sit again for days.

Dear Grandpapa – I see him yet
My friend, philosopher and guide, too,
A personality, once met,
One could not possibly forget,
Though lots of people tried to –
Founder of a distinguished line
And worthy ancestor of mine.

HARRY GRAHAM

Ragged-and-Tough

Ragged-and-Tough.

Not Ragged-and-Tough,
But –
    Huckem-a-Buff,
First cousin to Ragged-and-Tough.

Not Ragged-and-Tough
Nor Huckem-a-Buff
First cousin to Ragged-and-Tough,
But –
    Miss Grizzle,
Maiden aunt to Huckem-a-Buff
First cousin to Ragged-and-Tough.

Not Ragged-and-Tough
Nor Huckem-a-Buff
First cousin to Ragged-and-Tough
Nor Miss Grizzle, maiden aunt to Huckem-a-Buff
First cousin to Ragged-and-Tough,
But –

    Goody Gherkin,
Grandmama to Miss Grizzle
Maiden aunt to Huckem-a-Buff
First cousin to Ragged-and-Tough.

Not Ragged-and-Tough
Nor Huckem-a-Buff
First cousin to Ragged-and-Tough,
Nor Miss Grizzle, maiden aunt to Huckem-a-Buff
First cousin to Ragged-and-Tough,
Nor Goody Gherkin, grandmama to Miss Grizzle
Maiden aunt to Huckem-a-Buff
First cousin to Ragged-and-Tough,
But –
    Little Snap,
Favourite dog of Goody Gherkin
Grandmama to Miss Grizzle
Maiden aunt to Huckem-a-Buff
First cousin to Ragged-and-Tough.
Not Ragged-and-Tough
Nor Huckem-a-Buff
First cousin to Ragged-and-Tough,
Nor Miss Grizzle, maiden aunt to Huckem-a-Buff
First cousin to Ragged-and-Tough,
Nor Goody Gherkin, grandmama to Miss Grizzle
Maiden aunt to Huckem-a-Buff
First cousin to Ragged-and-Tough,
Nor Little Snap, favourite dog of Goody Gherkin
Grandmama to Miss Grizzle
Maiden aunt to Huckem-a-Buff
First cousin to Ragged-and-Tough,
But –
    the Whip,
Which tickled the tail of Little Snap,
Favourite dog of Goody Gherkin,
Grandmama to Miss Grizzle,
Maiden aunt to Huckem-a-Buff,
First cousin to Ragged-and-Tough.

ANONYMOUS

143

Great-Uncle Ben

My great-uncle Ben was the meanest of men,
   He would never let go of a dollar;
As a grudging resort, he made use of a wart
   On his neck, as a stud for his collar.
He would pasture his cows on the grave of his spouse,
   He would rob a blind babe of its bottle,
And he spoke through his nose, with a voice like a crow's,
   To avoid wear and tear to his throttle.
But he died, worth a million, intensely respected
By all who divided the wealth he'd collected.

The Moral, of course, is to work like a horse,
   And to save ev'ry coin you can muster,
That your sons who survive, though they loathed you alive,
   Round your deathbed may hopefully cluster.

HARRY GRAHAM

144

Learning

To Teach the H

Has Harry hopped over the hedge, Ann?
Has Albert felt hot in the air?
Ah, hand him to Hodge at the edge, Ann,
And hang up his hat on his hair.

Has Edith hired hampers for all, Ann?
Has Alice ate half of the eels?
Has Oswald his horse in the hall, Ann,
To hold up his elegant heels?

Has Ernest had all Harold had, Ann?
His egg and his herring to eat?
Is anything here he can add, Ann,
And have it at animal heat?

JENNETT HUMPHREYS

Froggy Gibberish

Whatever the phrase that the native may hurl, it's
Never the one that you picked up from Berlitz.

FELICIA LAMPORT

Lines Composed
in Fifth Row Centre

Of all the kinds of lecturer
   The lecturer I most detest
Is he who finishes a page
   And places it behind the rest.

I much prefer the lecturer
   Who takes the pages as he finishes
And puts them on a mounting pile
   As the original pile diminishes.

But best of all the lecturer
   Who gets his papers in confusion
And prematurely lets escape
   The trumpet-phrase: 'And in conclusion...'

MAURICE BISHOP

Brooklynese Champion

I thought the winner had been found
   The day I heard a woman make
The butcher cut her off a pound
   Of fine and juicy soylern steak.

Imagine then the dizzy whirl
   That through my head did swiftly surge
The day I heard the gifted girl
   Who wished departing friends 'Bon Verge.'

MARGARET FISHBACK

147

Response

Dear Brownjohn,

    Since you wrote me on behalf of the World Centre for Shakespeare Studies and asked if I'd be interested in contributing to 'Poems for Shakespeare, (and I said O.K.) I have had nine nights of recurrent nightmare wherein I balls up Act I Scene 2 thus:

'...Caesar said to me, "Dar'st thou, Cassius, now
Leap in with me into this angry flood,
And swim to yonder point?" Upon the word,
Accoutred as I was, I plungèd in,
And bade him follow: so, indeed, he did.
The torrent roar'd; and we did buffet it
With lusty sinews, throwing it aside,
And stemming it with hearts of controversy:
But ere we could arrive the point propos'd,
Caesar cried, "Dar'st thou, Cassius, now
Leap in with me into this angry flood,
And swim to yonder point?" Upon the word,
Accoutred as I was, I plungèd in,
And bade him follow: so, indeeed, he did.
The torrent roar'd: and we did buffet it
With lusty sinews, throwing it aside,
And stemming it with hearts of controversy:
But ere we could arrive the point propos'd,
Caesar cried, "Dar'st thou, Cassius, now
Leap in with me into this angry flood,
And swim to yonder point?" Upon the word,
Accoutred as I was, I plungèd in,
And bade him follow: so, indeed, he did.
The torrent roar'd; and we did buffet it
With lusty sinews, throwing it aside,
And stemming it with hearts of controversy:
But ere we could arrive the point propos'd,
Caesar cried, "Dar'st thou, Cassius, now..."'

I am imprisoned centrifugally
the Globe spins and the Gods are hissing 'OFF!'
those in the cheap seats who're not bored are angry
the trapdoor in the planks suddenly yawns
Caesar cries 'Help me, Cassius, or I sink!'
I am with dust and other discarded props
beneath the stage where real depth is cardboard
the Capitol is brittle polystyrene
my heart is in the coffin there with Caesar
I lick ash from the sockets of dry skull
this is not how I had envisaged it

– not, I imagine, what you had in mind.
I think perhaps you'd better count me out.

PETER READING

Oliver Wendell Holmes Slips Up

Down fell that pretty innocent, as falls a snow-white
     lamb;
Her hair drooped round her pallid cheeks, like seaweed
     on a clam.

OLIVER WENDELL HOLMES

A Riddle

A word there is of plural number
Foe to ease and tranquil slumber.
Any other word you take
And add an s will plural make;
But if you add an s to this
So strange the metamorphosis:
Plural is plural now no more
And sweet what bitter was before.

GEORGE CANNING

CARES

The Lesson

Of all the fleas that ever flew
  (And flying fleas are rather few
((Because for proper flying you
(((Whether you are a flea or not)))
Need wings and things fleas have not got)))–
(I make the further point that fleas
Are thick as these parentheses
((An illustration (((you'll agree)))
Both apt and pleasing to a flea)))–

Now then where were we? Let me see–
Ah, yes, – We said to fly you ought
(Whether you are a flea or not)
To have some wings (yes, at least two
((At least no less than two will do
(((And fleas have something less than one
((((One less, in fact (((((or, frankly, none
((((((Which, as once more you will agree))))))
Limits the flying of a flea))))))))))))))).
And let me add that fleas that fly
Are known as Flears. (You can see why.)
All I have said thus far is true
(If it's not clear, that's up to you.
((You'll have to learn sometime, my dear,
That what is true may not be clear
(((While what is clear may not be true
((((And you'll be wiser when you do.)))))))))).

JOHN CIARDI

151

Death of a Scrabble Master

This was the greatest of the game's great players:
If you played BRAS, he'd make it HUDIBRASTIC.
He ruled a world 15 by 15 squares,
Peopled by 100 letters, wood or plastic.

He unearthed XEBEC, HAJI, useful QAID,
Found QUOS (see pl. of QUID PRO QUO) and
    QUOTHA,
Discovered AU, DE, DA all unitalicized
(AU JUS, DA CAPO, ALMANACH DE GOTHA).

Two-letter words went marching through his brain,
Spondaic-footed, singing their slow litany:
AL (Indian mulberry), AI (a sloth), EM, EN,
BY, MY, SAZ, EX, OX, LO, IT, AN, HE...

PE (Hebrew letter), LI (Chinese mile), KA,RE,
SH (like NTH, spectacularly vowelless),
AY, OY (a cry of grief, pain or dismay);
HA, HI, HO – leaving opponents powerless.

He, if the tiles before him said DOC TIME,
Would promptly play the elegant DEMOTIC,
And none but he fulfilled the scrabbler's dream,
When, through two triple words, he hung QUIXOTIC.

The day his adversary put down GNASHED,
He laid – a virtuoso feat – beneath it GOUTIER,
So placed that six more tiny words were hatched:
GO NU, AT, SI, then (as you've seen, no doubt) HE, ER.

Plagued by a glut of U's, he racked up TUMULUS,
Produced ILLICIT when he had a boom in I's.
When once he couldn't hang his pretty AZIMUTH,
He found a dangling E, created HUMANIZE!

Receive him, EARTH (HEART's anagram is there);
His memory all players BLEES (var., BLESS, Scot.).
Inscribe his CENOTAPH (CAT PHONE) "I ACTS
    QUEER,"
for which he would of course read "REQUIESCAT."

CLEMENT BIDDLE WOOD

Nomenclaturik

There was a young fellow named Cholmondeley,
Whose bride was so mellow and colmondeley
That the best man, Coilquhoun,
An inane young bolqufoun,
Could only stand still and stare dolmondeley.

The bridegroom's first cousin, young Belvoir,
Whose dad was a Lancashire welvoir,
Arrived with George Bohun
At just about nohun
When excitement was mounting to felvoir.

The vicar – his surname was Beauchamp –
Of marriage endeavoured to teauchamp,
While the bridesmaid, Miss Marjoribanks,
Played one or two harjoripranks;
But the shoe that she threw failed to reauchamp.

HARRY HEARSON

Let's have a Party

Reach down the Thesaurus, put the Roget
before us; send for the harlot, the street-girl,
the courtesan, adultress, advoutress, kept woman,
the strumpet, the prostitute, the tart
and the broad, the hussy, the trollop, the jade, bitch and wh
send for the whole of the frail
sisterhood, and we'll have a cocktail
a party and food in a gigantic reception
a schnozzle, a rort, and that's no deception, no falsehood,
no imposture, no untruth, no conjure, no joke;
invite all the youngsters, the young-people,-folk,
the youths and the boys, the lads, slips
and callants and lassies and wenches and virgins and damsels
and colleens and flappers and hoydens and tomboys,
codlins and tadpoles and cublets and striplings to indulge
in some drinking, imbibing and tippling,
in boozing and toping
and swilling and soaking, bousing, carousing,
guzzling and swigging, draining and bibbing,
lushing and sponging till we all get drunk,
tipsy and temulent, inebri -ous, -ated, sewed up,
befuddled, intoxicated, obfuscated, maudlin and mellow,
groggy and beery; drunk as a piper, a fiddler,
a Chloe, squiffy and plastered and flustered,
musty and bosky, muddled and merry
and fou, fresh and fuddled,

so we'll wake up next morning
all twitching with pain, with headaches and toothaches,
migraine, neuralgia, neuritis, lumbago and gout,
tonsilitis, the tick, aching all over with spasms
cricks, stitches and kinks; with itches,
orgasms and soreness
and redness and rawness of all our blood plasms;
convulsions and throbbing, torment, torture, discomfort
and pangs; in anguish, in agony, with twinges that come
from going on binges and having such fun as
writing poems like this and exclaiming in chorus:
"What a wonderful thing is a Thesaurus!"

DON LAYCOCK

The Old Woman
and the Sandwiches

I met a wizened wood-woman
    Who begged a crumb of me:
Having four sandwiches to hand
    I gave her three.

"Bless you, thank you, kindly miss,
    Shall be rewarded well –
Three everlasting gifts, whose value
    None can tell."

"Three wishes?" out I cried in glee –
    "No, gifts you may not choose:
A flea and gnat to bit your back
    And gravel in your shoes."

LIBBY HOUSTON

Animals

Proverb

A bird in the hand is worth two in the wood:
For birdcatchers, maybe: for birds not so good.

Fishes' Nocturnal Ditty

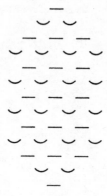

CHRISTIAN MORGERNSTERN

Sergeant Brown's Parrot

Many policemen wear upon their shoulders
Cunning little radios. To pass away the time
They talk about the traffic to them, listen to the news,
And it helps them to Keep Down Crime.

But Sergeant Brown, he wears upon his shoulder
A tall green parrot as he's walking up and down
And all the parrot says is 'Who's-a-pretty-boy-then?'
'I am', says Sergeant Brown.

KIT WRIGHT

A Three-Toed Tree Toad's Ode

A tree toad loved a she toad
  That lived high in a tree.
She was a two-toed tree toad
But a three-toed toad was he.

The three-toed tree toad tried to win
  The she toad's nuptial nod;
For the three-toed tree toad loved the road
The two-toed tree toad trod.

Hard as the three-toed tree toad tried,
  He could not reach her limb.
From her tree toad bower, with her V–toe power
The she toad vetoed him.

ANONYMOUS

The Honey Bee

the honey bee is sad and cross
and wicked as a weasel
and when she perches on your boss
she leaves a little measle

DON MARQUIS

Couplet for a Dog's Collar

I am his Highness' Dog at Kew;
Pray tell me Sir, whose Dog are you?

ALEXANDER POPE

Couplet for a Gamekeeper's Collar

I am his Lordship's dog at Whiteham,
And whom he bids me bite, I bite 'em.

GEORGE HUDDESFORD

The Cuckoo

In April the Cuckoo can sing her song by rote,
In June out of tune she cannot sing a note.
At first, cuckoo, cuckoo, sing still she can do,
At last, cuc, cuc, cuc, six cucs to one koo.

JOHN HEYWOOD

Good Luck

There was once a brainy baboon,
Who always breathed down a bassoon,
For he said, 'It appears
That in billions of years
I shall certainly hit on a tune.'

SIR ARTHUR STANLEY EDDINGTON

Offer it Up

He prayeth best who loveth best
All creatures great and small.
The Streptococcus is the test
I love him least of all.

ANONYMOUS

The Decision

On a mudflat by a river
Near the Bay of Apropos,
Sat a Quagga all aquiver
Filling reticules with snow,
When she noticed someone sulky
Locomoting down the shore,
Someone somewhat grey and bulky,
Though 'twas only five to four.
Said that Quagga: "'Tis the Sheep –
Late again, and fast asleep!
Doubtless, as my friend and neighbour,
He will ask me why I labour
Filling reticules with snow.
But I shall not tell him. No!"

ANONYMOUS

The Loch Ness Monster's Song

Sssnnnwhuffffll?
Hnwhuffl hhnnwlf hnfl hfl?
Gdroblboblhobngbl gbl gl g g g g glbgl.
Drublhaflablhaflubhafgabhaflhafl fl fl–
gm grawwwww grf grawf awfgm graw gm.
Hovoplodok-doplodovok-plovodokot-doplodokosl
Splgraw fok fok splgrafhatchgabrlgabrl fok splfok!
Zgra kra gka fok!
Grof grawff gahf?
Gombl mbl bl –
blm plm,
blm plm, glm plm,
blp.

EDWIN MORGAN

The Hen

Higgledy-piggledy
My white hen,
She lays eggs for gentlemen;
You cannot persuade her with gun or lariat
To come across for the proletariat.

DOROTHY PARKER

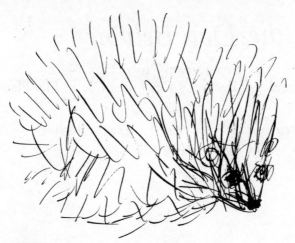

The Happy Hedgehog

The happiness of hedgehogs
  Lies in complete repose.
They spend the months of winter
  In a long delicious doze;
And if they note the time at all
  They think 'How fast it goes!'

E.V. RIEU

Bull

Bull picked
Bull reared
Bull pricked
Bull feared

Bull run
Bull rated
Bull fun
Bull baited

Bull billed
Bull hit
Bull killed
Bull shit

TULI KUPFERBERG

To the Dog Belvoir

Whom I saw in a Dream Push Baby N.
from under a Brewer's Dray and Die in His Place

The stricken Belvoir raised a paw and said:
I die a perfect gentle quadruped.

STEVIE SMITH

Gilbert White

'Dinner-time?' said Gilbert White,
'Yes, yes – certainly – all right.
Just let me finish this note
About the Lesser White-bellied Stoat.'

E.C. BENTLEY

To a Timid Leech

Nay, start not from the banquet where the red wines
  foams for thee –
Though somewhat thick to perforate this epidermis be;
'Tis madness, when the bowl invites, to linger at the
  brink;
So haste thee, haste thee, timid one. Drink, pretty
  creature, drink!

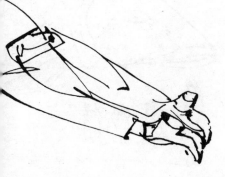

I tell thee, if these azure veins could boast the regal wine
Of Tudors or Plantagenets, the draught should still be
    thine!
Though round the goblet's beaded brim plebeian
    bubbles wink,
'Twill cheer and not inebriate. Drink, pretty creature,
    drink!

Perchance, reluctant being, I have placed thee wrong
    side up,
And the lips that I am chiding have been farthest from
    the cup,
I have waited long and vainly, and I cannot, cannot
    think
Thou wouldst spurn the oft-repeated call: Drink, pretty
    creature, drink!

While I watch'd thy patient struggles, and imagined
    thou were coy,
'Twas thy tail, and not thy features, that refused the
    proffer'd joy,
I will but turn thee tenderly – nay, never, never shrink –
Now, once again the banquet calls: Drink, pretty
    creature drink!

HENRY SAMBROOKE LEIGH

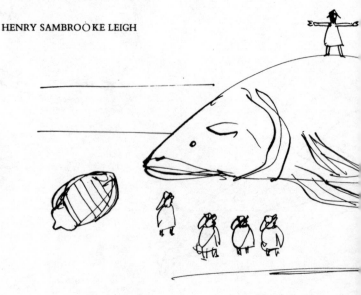

The Fisherman's Prayer

O give me grace to catch a fish
  So big that even I,
In talking of it afterwards,
  May have no need to lie.

ANONYMOUS

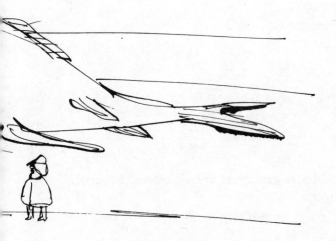

Food & Drink

The local groceries are all out of broccoli,
Loccoli.

ROY BLOUNT, JNR.

I Take 'Em and Like 'Em

I'm fonder of carats than carrots,
  And orchids are nicer than beans,
But life in a series of garrets
  Has made me receptive to greens.

MARGARET FISHBACK

Hints on Table Etiquette

To a Baked Fish

Preserve a respectful demeanor
  When you are brought into the room,
Don't stare at the guests while they're eating
  No matter how much they consume.

To Lettuce

The humblest are counted the wisest,
  The modest are lauded the most;
Don't have a big head because sometimes
  You sit on the right of the host.

To a Salad

The lady whose costume is smartest
  May not be the most honored guest;
Don't think you are better than others
  Because you are very well dressed.

CAROLYN WELLS

The Chavender, or Chub

There is a fine stuffed chavender,
  A chavender or chub,
That decks the rural pavender,
  The pavender or pub,
Wherein I eat my gravender,
  My gravender or grub.

How good the honest gravender!
  How snug the rustic pavender!
From sheets as sweet as lavender,
  As lavender, or lub,
I jump into my tavender,
  My tavender, or tub.

Alas! for town and clavender,
  For business and club!
They call me from my pavender
To-night; ay, there's the ravender,
  Ay, there comes in the rub!
To leave each blooming shravender,
  Each spring-bedizened shrub,
And meet the horsy savender,
  The very forward sub,
At dinner at the clavender,
And then at billiards dravender,
  At billiards roundly drub
The self-sufficient cavender
  The not ill-meaning cub,
Who me a bear will davender,
  A bear unfairly dub,
Because I sometimes snavender,
  Not too severely snub,
His setting right the clavender,
  His teaching all the club!

Farewell to peaceful pavender,
   My river-dreaming pub,
To bed as sweet as lavender,
To homely, wholesome gravender,
And you, inspiring chavender,
   Stuff'd, chavender, or chub.

WARHAM ST. LEDGER

Epitaph on a Country Inn Destroyed by Fire

A fire has destroyed the Chameleon at Strood,
   Which makes me exceedingly glad;
For the waitresses there were disgustingly rude
   And the food was incredibly bad.

T. MICHAEL POPE

Athol Brose

Charm'd with a drink which Highlanders compose,
   A German traveller exclaim'd with glee –,
Potztausend! sare, if dis is Athol Brose,
   How goot dere Athol Boetry must be!

THOMAS HOOD

The Test

He is not drunk who, from the floor
Can rise again and drink some more;
But he is drunk who prostrate lies
And cannot drink, and cannot rise.

ANONYMOUS

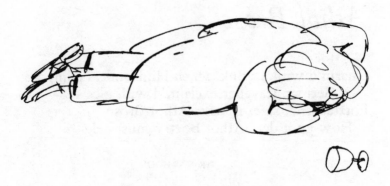

174

To a Fish of the Brook

Enjoy thy stream, O harmless fish;
And when an angler for his dish,
   Through gluttony's vile sin,
Attempts, a wretch, to pull thee out,
God give thee strength, O gentle trout,
      To pull the rascal in!

JOHN WOLCOT

Coffee

Sound the bugle and roll the drum!
Hail King Coffee, your hour is come!
Wreathed with chicory, lads and lasses,
Toast our monarch in demitasses.
Roast him, toast him, sing a glee!
To this merry old bean out of Araby.

Bacchus II his name and style,
Merry monarch of Java's isle.
He shall liven the revel late;
He shall addle the poet's pate;
Rule the dances of nymph and satyr,
Bubbling lord of the percolator.
Brew his Mocha and quaffing hot,
Burble, bards, of the perkling pot.

KEITH PRESTON

Water

A pint of Water
Weighs a Pound and a Quarter.

ANONYMOUS

Tomato Ketchup

If you do not shake the bottle,
None'll come, and then a lot'll.

ANONYMOUS

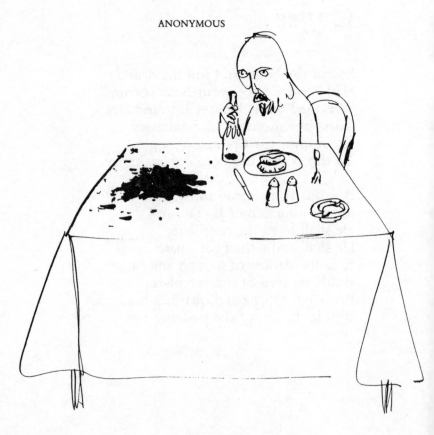

Lines for a Urinal Wall

I depend on the brewers,
And the brewers depend on me.
We all depend on the sewers
As they flow to the ancient sea,
   Where the wavelets dash
   And the bathers splash,
By a rusty Victorian pier.
   The trouble with this
   Is the sea's full of piss
   And not the original beer.

TEDDY SKINNER

Classes

As I sat down one evening
In a small café,
A forty-year-old waitress
These words to a man did say:

'I see you are a logger
And not just a common bum,
Because nobody but a logger
Stirs his coffee with his thumb.'

ANONYMOUS

The Ballad of William Bloat

In a mean abode in the Shankill Road
   Lived a man named William Bloat;
Now he had a wife, the plague of his life,
   Who continually got his goat,
And one day at dawn, with her night-shift on,
   He slit her bloody throat.

With razor-gash he settled her hash –
   Oh, never was death so quick:
But the steady drip on the pillowslip
   Of her life-blood turned him sick,
And the pool of gore on the bedroom floor
   Grew clotted and cold and thick.

Now he was right glad he had done as he had
   As his wife lay there so still,
When a sudden awe of the mighty Law
   Struck his heart with an icy chill,
And, to finish the fun so well begun,
   He resolved himself to kill.

He took the sheet from his wife's cold feet
   And knotted it into a rope,
And hanged himself from the pantry shelf –
   An easy death, let's hope.
In the jaws of death with his latest breath
   Said he, 'To Hell with the Pope.'

But the strangest turn of the whole concern
   Is only just beginning:
He went to Hell, but his wife got well
   And is still alive and sinning,
For the razor-blade was Dublin-made
   But the sheet was Belfast linen.

ANONYMOUS

The Shropshire Lads

When lads have done with labour
   in Shropshire, one will cry,
'Let's go and kill a neighbour,'
   and t'other answers 'Aye!'

So this one kills his cousins,
   and that one kills his dad;
and, as they hang by dozens
   at Ludlow, lad by lad,

each of them one-and-twenty,
   all of them murderers,
the hangman mutters: 'Plenty
   even for Housman's verse.'

HUMBERT WOLFE

The Old Barmaid

When Mrs Wellum first I knew
   Four teeth in all she reckoned;
Up comes a cough, and does for two,
   And t'other two, a second.

Courage! I cry, and never fear
   The third when'ere it comes;
Bring me another glass of bear
   And I'll adore you gums.

ANONYMOUS

The Secretary

When I go out to lunch at one,
Aware that I must eat, and run
Back to the desk from whence I sprang,
The Moodiest orang-outang
Alive is sweet compared to me.
For every time I'm forced to see
Coveys of females on their way
To view a mid-week matinée,
My inclination is to tear
Them limb from limb and hair from hair.

MARGARET FISHBACK

Edinburgh Scene

we used to be typists
but the hell wi' that
now we live with these boys
in a two room flat

we've never washed for ages
we sleep on bits of sack
we've baith lost wir pants
and wi dannae want them back

the boys are a' big beardies
they think we're awfy sweet
we never know which one we're with
that's what it means to be beat

ALAN JACKSON

The Builders

Good Mr. Ware came down with all his men,
  And filled the house with lovely oily pails,
And went away to lunch at half-past ten,
  And came again at tea-time with some nails.

A. P. HERBERT

The Famous Ballad of the Jubilee Cup

You may lift me up in your arms, lad, and turn my
    face to the sun,
For a last look back at the dear old track where the
    Jubilee cup was won;
And draw your chair to my side, lad – no, thank ye,
    I feel no pain –
For I'm going out with the tide, lad; but I'll tell you
    the tale again.

'Twas a nine-hole thresh to wind'ard (but none of us
    cared for that),
With a straight run home to the service tee, and a
    finish along the flat,
'Stiff?' ah, well you may say it! Spot barred, and at
    five stone ten!
But at two and a bisque I'd ha' run the risk; for I was
    a greenhorn then.

John Roberts (scratch), and Safety Match, The Lascar,
    and Lorna Doone,
Oom Paul (a bye), and Romany Rye, and me upon
    Wooden Spoon:
And I leaned and patted her centre-bit and eased the
    quid in her cheek,
With a 'Soh my lass!' and a 'Woa you brute' – for
    she could do all but speak.

She was geared a thought too high perhaps; she was
    trained a trifle fine;
But she had the grand reach forward! I never saw such a
    line!
Smooth-bored, clean run, from her fiddle head with its
    dainty ear half-cock,
Hard-bit, pur sang, from her overhang to the heel of
    her off hind sock.

Sir Robert he walked beside me as I worked her down
    to the mark;
'There's money on this, my lad,' said he, 'and most of
    'em running dark;
But ease the sheet if you're bunkered, and pack the
    scrummages tight,
And use your slide at the distance, and we'll drink to
    your health to-night!'

But I bent and tightened my stretcher. Said I to myself,
    said I–
'John Jones, this here is the Jublilee Cup, and you
    have to do or die.'
And the words weren't hardly spoken when the umpire
    shouted 'Play!'
And we all kicked off from the Gasworks End with a
    'Yoicks!' and a 'Gone Away!'

The Lascar made the running but he didn't amount
    to much,
For old Oom Paul was quick on the ball, and headed
    it back to touch;
And the whole first flight led off with the right as The
    Saint took up the pace,
And drove it clean to the putting green and trumped
    it there with an ace.

John Roberts had given a miss in baulk, but Villa
    cleared with a punt;
And keeping her service hard and low the Meteor
    forged to the front;
With Romany Rye to the windward at dormy and two
    to play,
And Yale close up – but a Jubilee Cup isn't run for
    every day.

It was bellows to mend with Roberts – starred three
for a penalty kick:
But he chalked his cue and gave 'em the butt, and Oom
Paul marked the trick–
'Offside – No ball – and at fourteen all! Mark Cock!
and two for his nob!'
When W. G. ran clean through his lee and beat him
twice with a lob.

He yorked him twice on a crumbling pitch and wiped
his eye with a brace,
But his guy-rope split with the strain of it and he
dropped back out of the race;
And I drew a bead on the Meteor's lead, and
challenging none too soon,
Bent over and patted her garboard strake, and called
upon Wooden Spoon.

So, inch by inch, I tightened the winch, and chucked
the sandbags out –
I heard the nursery cannons pop, I heard the bookies
shout:
'The Meteor wins!' 'No, Wooden Spoon!', 'Check!'
'Vantage!' 'Leg Before!'
'Last Lap!' 'Pass Nap!' At his saddle-flap I put up
the helm and wore.

Had I lost at that awful juncture my presence of mind?
...but no!
I leaned and felt for the puncture and plugged it there
with my toe...
Hand over hand by the Members' Stand I lifted and
eased her up,
Shot – clean and fair – to the crossbar there, and landed
the Jubilee Cup!

'The odd by a head, and leg before,' so the Judge he
    gave the word:
And the umpire shouted 'Over!' but I neither spoke
    nor stirred.
They crowded round: for there on the ground I lay in
    a dead–cold swoon,
Pitched neck and crop on the turf atop of my beautiful
    Wooden Spoon.

Her dewlap tire was punctured, her bearings all red
    hot;
She'd a lolling tongue, and her bowsprit sprung, and
    her running gear in a knot;
And amid the sobs of her backers, Sir Robert loosened
    her girth
And led her away to the knacker's. She had raced her
    last on earth!

I'm going out with the tide, lad – you'll dig me a
    numble grave,
And whiles you will bring your bride, lad, and your
    sons, if sons you have,
And there when the dews are weeping, and the echoes
    murmur 'Peace!'
And the salt, salt tide comes creeping and covers the
    popping-crease;

In the hour when the ducks deposit their eggs with a
    boasted force,
They'll look and whisper 'How was it?' and you'll
    take them over the course,
And your voice will break as you try to speak of the
    glorious first of June,
When the Jubilee Cup, with John Jones up, was won
    upon Wooden Spoon.

SIR ARTHUR T. QUILLER-COUCH

A Gentleman of the Old School

Here lies a man of wealth and rank
Who hunted, whored, made bets and drank:
There is not much to tell beside
Except that he was born and died.

COLIN ELLIS

A Gentleman of the New School

Here lies his son, who lacked the skill,
To live magnificently ill,
And loathed, while failing to avoid,
The follies that his sire enjoyed.

COLIN ELLIS

Foot baller

On a wooden

pink,

American,

stands.

padded head, he

wooden pole

which are a

painted footballs.

push him, he

on his poised

however hard you

hit his wooden pole, or

ends of his pole,he

loses his balance, but

rocks to

weight from one

other

he regains his

with a delicate

tippety-tap, he

to a neat

pillar, a

leaning,

footballer,

Above his

holds a

on the ends of

pair of

When you

sways, jigs

wooden feet, and,

hit him, or

hit the footballs on the

never topples, or

only slowly

and fro, tilting his

foot to the

until

balance, and then

tip-tap

dances

halt.

GEORGE
MACBETH

The Quatrains for Lady Cabstanleigh

The Borough Councillors Sing to Lady Cabstanleigh

She is so large she blocks the light,
She's like a huge obstructing wall.
Let's pull her down and use the site
To build ourselves a new Town Hall.

Lady Cabstanleigh in Amateur Theatricals

Oh, touch the harp, bid solemn music sound,
   Enter the Fairy Queen, a bit unstable.
Dragging one massive foot along the ground,
   And flying on a forty-inch steel cable.

For Lady Cabstanleigh's Birthday

Oh, see the massive scale my lady's built on
She is the ground-plan for a mammoth Stilton.
Or, upon days when her great face is redder,
The blue-print for a more gigantic Cheddar.

J. B. MORTON

The Justice of the Peace

Distinguish carefully between these two,
   This thing is yours, that other thing is mine.
You have a shirt, a brimless hat, a shoe
   And half a coat. I am the Lord benign
Of fifty hundred acres of fat land
To which I have a right. You understand?

I have a right because I have, because,
   Because I have – because I have a right.
Now be quite calm and good, obey the laws,
   Remember your low station, do not fight
Against the goad, because, you know, it pricks,
Whenever the uncleanly demos kicks.

I do not envy you your hat, your shoe.
   Why should you envy me my small estate?
It's fearfully illogical in you
   To fight with economic force and fate.
Moreover, I have got the upper hand,
And mean to keep it. Do you understand?

HILAIRE BELLOC

Bust

A monster, in a course of vice grown old,
Leaves to his gaping heir his ill-gain'd gold;
Straight breathes his bust, straight are his virtues shown,
Their date commencing with a sculptur'd stone.

If on his specious marble we rely,
Pity a worth like his should ever die!
If credit to his real life we give,
Pity a wretch like him should ever live!

SAMUEL WESLEY

L was a Lady, Advancing in Age

L was a Lady, Advancing in Age,
  Who drove in her carriage and six,
With a Couple of Footmen, a Coachman and Page,
  Who were all of them regular bricks.
If the Coach ran away, or was smashed by a Dray,
  Or got into collisions and blocks,
The Page, with a courtesy rare for his years,
  Would leap to the ground with inspiriting cheers,
While the Footman allayed her legitimate fears,
  And the Coachman sat tight on his box.
At night as they met round an excellent meal,
  They would take it in turn to observe:
'What a Lady indeed!..what a presence to feel!..'
  'What a Woman to worship and serve!...'
But, perhaps, the most poignant of all their delights
  Was to stand in a rapturous Dream
When she spoke to them kindly on Saturday Nights,
  And said 'They deserved her Esteem.'

MORAL

Now observe the Reward of these dutiful lives:
  At the end of their Loyal Career
They each had a Lodge at the end of the drives,
  And she left them a Hundred a Year.
Remember from this to be properly vexed
  When the newspaper editors say,
That 'The type of society shown in the Text
  Is rapidly passing away.'

HILIARE BELLOC

High-Life Low-Down

To his Castle Lord Fothergay bore his young bride,
And he carried her over the drawbridge so wide,
Through the Great Hall, the Solar, the West Hall, the East,
And thirty-eight principal bedrooms at least,
Up seventeen stairways and down many more
To a basement twelve yards by a hundred and four,
And at last set her down – he was panting a bit –
In front of the sink and said "Kid, this is IT."

JUSTIN RICHARDSON

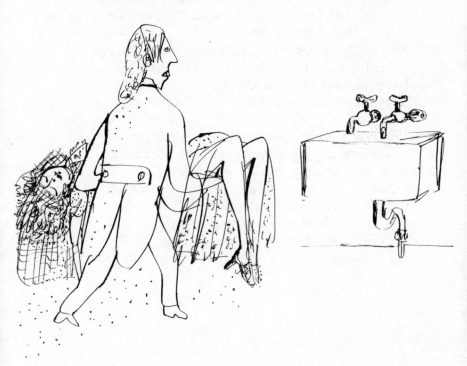

Good Byron

A note on The Vision of Judgement

Nor did I spare from commination that
   Corpulent Hanoverian, the Fourth George.
Though hard to pierce, through the thick layers of fat
   That, blubberlike, protected him – his gorge
Felt my harpoon, and much he winced thereat;
   Had it been mine the bolts of Jove to forge,
I would have sent a dozen down to brighten
This mean Sardanapalus out of Brighton!

Enough: I leave my poems and my fame
   To calmer judgment than in life they met.
If, in my writing, of the sacred flame
   Some sparks were burning, and are burning yet,
I think I have made out a decent claim
   That England will not readily forget.
To rank amongst her singers; – if excluded,
I still wrote better, Southey, far, than you did.

WILLIAM PROWSE

The Lady of Leigh

'Misery me!'
  Said the Lady of Leigh,
    As she queued for a bus in the Strand,
And callous conductresses, weary of work,
Drifted disdainfully into the murk
  With a laugh at her lily-white hand.
'Oh the ladylike ease at Leigh on the Sea!
The curtains and comfort, the toast and the tea!
There goes another one – misery me!
      Misery Me!'
    Said the Lady of Leigh.

E. V. RIEU

Lines on Lord Pembroke's Whitewashing the Back of
his House Beside the Thames

Upon the Thames I daily rowed
Full twenty years or thirty,
Where Pembroke's earl his backside showed
Black, yellow, brown, and dirty.

But lately, as I passed, I cried
(So white and clean it made is),
Ashamed at last of his backside
His Lordship shows his Ladies.

BY A WATERMAN

It is said that John Wilmot, the 2nd Earl of Rochester, pinned the following rhyme to door of Charles II bedroom:

> Here lies our sovereign lord the King,
> Whose word no man relies on;
> Who never said a foolish thing
> And never did a wise one.

To which Charles is said to have replied:

> Ah, witty Wilmot, I obeyed
> Those clamorous submissions
> That left my words my own but made
> My acts, my politicians.

When Charles II
Beckoned
Nell
    Fell.

RUTH SILCOCK

Exit

Plingen, plangen, aufgefangen,
　Swingen, swangen at my side,
Pootle, swootle, off to Bootle,
　Nemesis, a pleasant ride.

MALCOLM LOWRY

Actuarial Reflection

Very, very, very few
People die at ninety-two.
I suppose that I shall be
Safer still at ninety-three.

WILLARD R. ESPY

The Undertaker's Advertisement

Why pay more for your funeral when
We've put away far better men,
Coffin and all, for twelve pounds and ten?

And this about your friends? Their pride?
Because the coffin's only dyed
To look like maple? You inside

May rest secure – our guarantee –
That no man ever made so free
As to scratch a coffin's lid to see!

ERNEST G. MOLL

The Corpse's Song

Down among the sainted dead
   Many years I lay;
Beetles occupied my head,
   Moles explored my clay.

There we feasted day and night –
   I and bug and beast;
They provided appetite
   And I supplied the feast.

AMBROSE BIERCE

Unanswered Prayer

There was aince an auld body o' Sydney
Wha suffered frae pains in the kidney.
    He prayed tae the Lord
    That he micht be restored,
And He promised He would – but He didnae!

ANONYMOUS

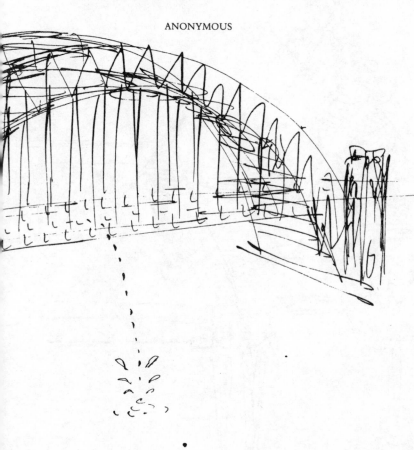

Dear Messrs. Tippins

Dear Messrs. Tippins, what is feared by you,
Alas! the melancholy circumstance is true,
That I am dead! And more afflicting still,
My legal assets cannot pay your bill!
To think of this I'm almost broken-hearted –
Insolvent I this earthly life departed!
Dear Messrs. T., I'm yours without a farthing.
For executors and self.

GEORGE HARDING

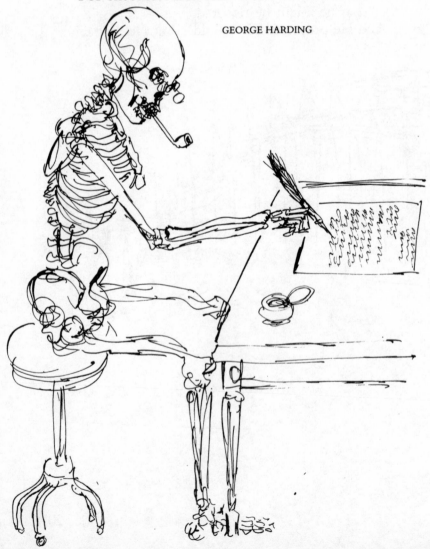

The Sexton's Song

sung by Ben Jonson while playing the Gravedigger in Hamlet.

Once more to my Arms, my dear pickaxe, my spade,
And the other fine tools that belong to my trade;
O the higher they lived, the deeper they're laid.
　Ring-a-ding, ring-a-ding, ring-a-ding-a-ding-ding!

Or ravaged with palsy; or raddled by gout,
If rabble or royal, if dammed or devout,
What door you came in by, this door you'll go out.
　Ring-a-ding, ring-a-ding, ring-a-ding-a-ding-ding!

At christenings I drink to the girl or the boy,
And pray that they neither be mine to employ
Before they are hoyden or hobbledehoy.
　Ring-a-ding, ring-a-ding, ring-a-ding-a-ding-ding.

So bless you, my neighbours; and come by-and-by,
Get married, have children, then decently die;
No tradesman will use you as gently as I.
　Ring-a-ding, ring-a-ding, ring-a-ding,-a-ding-ding!

ANONYMOUS

On John Camden Hotten

Hotten,
Rotten,
Forgotten.

GEORGE AUGUSTUS SALA

203

Miss Bailey

A Captain bold from Halifax who dwelt in country
    quarters,
Betrayed a maid who hanged herself one morning
    in her Garters.
His wicked conscience smited him, he lost his
    Stomach daily.
And took to drinking Ratafia while thinking of Miss
    Bailey.

One night betimes he went to bed, for he had
    caught a Fever;
Says he, 'I am a handsome man, but I'm a gay
    Deceiver.'
His candle just at twelve o'clock began to burn
    quite palely,
A Ghost stepped up to his bedside and said
    'Behold Miss Bailey!'

'Avant, Miss Bailey!' then he cries 'your Face
    looks white and mealy.'
'Dear Captain Smith,' the ghost replied, 'you've
    used me ungenteelly;
The Crowner's 'Quest goes hard with me because
    I've acted frailly,
And Parson Biggs won't bury me though I am
    dead Miss Bailey.'

'Dear Corpse!' said he, 'since you and I
    accounts must once for all close,
There really is a one pound note in my regimental
    Smallclothes;
I'll bribe the sexton for your grave.' The ghost
    then vanished gaily
Crying 'Bless you, Wicked Captain Smith,
    Remember poor Miss Bailey.'

ANONYMOUS

Le Revenant

My Uncle from the realms of Death
Returned to draw an earthly breath
And as he walked upon the heath
The wild wind whistled through his teeth.

He came unto a habitation
That was the centre of the nation
He knocked upon each house and said:
It is much better to be dead.

And when they stoned him from the door
He vowed he would come back no more.

STEVIE SMITH

Nemo's Farewell

I was once on the table; I'm now on the shelf.
Let me give a look round, and take stock of myself.
We are not a large party: an ancient Who's Who
(Grim sepulchre now of some names that were new!)
Spectator, vol. four, and a Scot's Magazine,
With a bulky Burn's Justice wedged tightly between;
The excellent Hanway, his Essay on Tea,
And Rhymes for the Roadway – by 'Nemo'. That's Me!

AUSTIN DOBSON

On Myself

Here lies the body of Edith Bone.
All her life she lived alone,
Until Death added the final S
And put an end to her loneliness.

EDITH BONE

Acknowledgements

It is my pleasure to thank Mr Peter Marcan, the compiler of *Poetry Themes*, for the many pointers contained in that bibliography, and for introducing me to the *Catalog of the Schmulowitz Collection of Wit and Humor*; Mr Willard R. Espy, the author and compiler of *An Almanac of–* and *Another Almanac of Words at Play*, and Mr Simon Brett, the compiler of *The Faber Book of Useful Verse*, anthologies from which I have taken several items; and Mrs A. V. House of the Canada House Library who helped me discover several out-of-the-way books: thereafter, the Staff of the Reading Room, the British Library; Mr Douglas Matthew and the Staff of the London Library; Mr Jonathan Barker of the Arts Council Poetry Library: Mr John Cowell of the Victoria Library, London Borough of Westminster; the Staff of the library, the University of London: the Staff of the library, the Library Association; Mr Basil Boothroyd, Mr Richard Adams of the Open Head Press, Mr Clive Bingley, Ms Carmen Calill, Mr Peter Clarke, Mr Samuel Carr, Mr William Cookson of *Agenda*, Mr André Deutsch, Ms Faith Eckler of *Word Ways*, Mr Bamber Gascoigne, Mr Charles Graham, Mr James Greene, Mrs Kate Grimmond, Mr Michael Hastings, Mr Richard Ingrams, Ms Ruth Keonig, Mr Dennis Lee, Mr Jay Landesman, Mr Edward Lucie-Smith, Mr George Melly, Mr Blake Morrison, Mr Brian Patten, Miss Jennifer Patterson, Ms Stephanie Pixner, Mr Tony Rushton, Miss Elizabeth Ritchie, Mr Derek Stanford, Mr Simon Watson Taylor, Mr J. J. Webster, Mr Heathcote Williams, and Mr Peter Watson of *The Times*.

Barrington, Patrick, *Take me in Your Arms Miss Moneypenny-Wilson* from SONGS OF A SUB-MAN, Patrick Barrington. Reprinted by permission of Methuen, London.

Beerbohm, Max, *Milton* from MAX IN VERSE (ed. J.G. Riewald), published by William Heineman Ltd.

Belfrage, Sally, *Progress* from JIGGERY-POKERY (ed. Anthony Hecht & John Hollander). Reprinted by permission of the author.

Belloc, Hilaire, *The Pacifist, The Justice of the Peace, Aunt Jane* and *L Was a Lady Advancing in Age* from COLLECTED POEMS. Reprinted by permission of Gerald Duckworth and Company ltd.

Bentley, E.C., *Gilbert White* from THE COMPLETE CLERIHEWS OF E. CLERIHEW BENTLEY (1981). Reprinted by permission of Oxford University Press.

Bishop, Maurice, *Lines Composed in Fifth Row Centre*, published by The Dial Press.

Blount Jnr, Roy, 'The Local groceries are all out of broccoli' in ATLANTIC MONTHLY (1941). Reprinted by permission of International Creative Management Inc, New York.

Bone, Edith, *On Myself* from THE FABER BOOK OF NONSENSE VERSE (ed. G. 'Grouser' Grigson). Reprinted by permission of Vera H. Black.

Brecht, Bertold (trans. John Willett) *X* from POEMS 1913-1956 (ed. John Willett and Ralph Manheim). Reprinted by permission of Methuen, London.

Catullus, Gaius Valerius (trans. Joseph Salemi), *Ameana* from CATULLUS: COMPLETE POEMS (ed. R. Myers and R. Ormesby). Reprinted by permission of George Allen & Unwin.

Chesterton, G.K., *Wind and Water* from THE COLLECTED POEMS OF G.K. CHESTERTON, published by Methuen, London. Reprinted by permission of Miss D.E. Collins.

Ciardi, John, *The Lesson* from AN ALMANAC OF WORKS AT PLAY (ed. Willard E. Espy), John Ciardi. Reprinted by permission of the author.

Cope, Wendy, *The Expense of Sprits is a Crying Shame* from STRUGNELL'S SONNETS, published in QUARTO: *Proverbial Ballade* from POETRY INTRODUCTION 5, published by Faber & Faber; and *Chimpanzee*. Reprinted by permission of the author.

Craddle, W., *On a Certain Scholar* from WHAT CHEER (ed. David McCord), published by Coward McCann (USA), 1945.

Cutler, Ivor, *Search for Grace* from A FLAT MAN, published by The Trigram Press Ltd, 1977.

Daly, T.A., *The Tides of Love* from SELECTED POEMS T.A. DALY, 1936. Reprinted by permission of Harcourt Brace Ltd.

Day, Clarence, *Who and What* and *The Ancient Way* from THOUGHTS WITHOUT WORDS, *Ape into Man, On Lido's Shore, A Friendly Soul* and *From Noah to Now* from AFTER ALL. Reprinted by permission of Alfred A Knopf Inc., New York.

Eddington, Arthur Stanley, *Good Luck* from NEW PATHWAYS IN SCIENCE, Sir Arthur Stanley Eddington, 1935. Reprinted by permission of Cambridge University Press.

Ellis, Colin, *To James Who Could Not Suffer Fools Gladly, International Conference, The Amateurs, Vice and Virtue, Epitaph on a Prig, A Gentleman of the Old School, A Gentleman of the New School* from MOURNFUL NUMBERS, Colin Ellis, 1931. Reprinted by permission of Macmillan, London and Basingstoke.

Espy, Willard R., *Acturial Reflection* from ANOTHER ALMANAC OF WORDS AT PLAY, Willard E. Espy, 1981. Reprinted by permission of André Deutsch Ltd.

Evans, E.J., *Mozart* from THE NEW STATESMAN COMPETITION WINNERS (ed. G.W. Stonier), published by Faber & Faber, 1946. Reprinted by permission of The New Statesman.

Ezekiel, Nissim, *The Patriot* from LATTERDAY PSALMS, 1982. Reprinted by permission of the Oxford University Press, India.

Fishback, Margaret, *Abracadabra, Natura in Urbe, I Take 'Em and Like 'Em, The Secretary* from I TAKE IT BACK by Margaret Fishback, 1935 by E.P. Dutton and Co Inc; renewal, 1963 by Margaret Fishback Antolini. *Brooklynese Champion* from OUT OF MY HEAD by Margaret Fishback, 1933 by E.P. Dutton & Co Inc; renewal, 1951 by Margaret Fishback Antolini. Reprinted by permission of the publisher.

Graham, Harry, *Grandpapa* from STRAINED RELATIONS, 1926, published by Methuen, London. *Great Uncle Ben* from CANNED CLASSICS, 1911, published by Mills & Boon.

Graves, Charles, *Mr Winston Churchill* from PARTY PORTRAITS, Charles Graves, 1910, published by Smith Elder & Co.

Graves, Robert, *A Slice of Wedding Cake* from COLLECTED POEMS, Robert Graves, 1975. Reprinted by permission of the author.

Guitterman, Arthur, 'Since one anthologist put in his book' from LYRIC LAUGHTER Arthur Guitterman, 1939. Reprinted by permission of Louise H. Sclove.

Hastings, Michael, *The Trip.* Reprinted by permission of the author.

Herbert, A.P., *I Can't Think What He Sees in Her* from A BOOK OF BALLADS, A.P. Herbert, 1931; and *The Builders* in PUNCH, 1919. Reprinted by permission of the Estate of the late Sir Alan Herbert.

Horovitz, Michael, *The Changing Face of an Actress* from GROWING UP, Michael Horovitz, 1979. Reprinted by permission of the author.

Houston, Libby, 'The Fisherman who cannot wait' from THE SAME; *It was not much but it was something* and *The Old Woman and the Sandwiches* from PLAIN CLOTHES, Libby Houston, 1971. Reprinted by permission of Allison & Busby.

Ingrams, Richard, *Lines on the Unmasking of the Surveyor of the Queen's Pictures* from PRIVATE EYE, 7/12/79. Reprinted by permission of the author.

Jackson, Alan, *Knox, Young Politician, Edinburgh Scene.* Reprinted by permission of the author.

Jandl, Ernst, *Oberflächenübersetzung* from MODERN POETRY IN TRANSLATION, 1971, Reprinted by permission of the author.

Johnston, George, *Life from a Goldfish Bowl* from THE CRUISING AUK, George Johnston, 1958. Reprinted by permission of the author.

Kaufman, Gerald Lynton, *Cellarithmetic* from GEO-METRIC VERSES, Gerald Lynton Kaufman, 1948, published by Barnes & Co.

Kipling, Rudyard, *My Rival* from DEPARTMENTAL DITTIES. Reprinted by permission of the National Trust.

Kupferberg, Tuli, *Bull* from LESS NEWSPOEMS, 1981. Reprinted by permission of the author.

Lamport, Felicia, *'Whatever the phrase that the native may hurl, its'* from SCRAP IRONY, 1962, published by the Houghton Mifflin Company. Reprinted by permission of the author.

Lebrun, Ponce-Denis Ecouchard, *(trans. George Rostrevor Hamilton), 'This poet in a lifetime all too short O'* from WIT'S LOOKING GLASS, published by William Heinemann Ltd.

Logue, Christopher, *To a Friend in Search of Rural Seclusion When All Else Fails* from ODE TO THE DODO, Christopher Logue. Reprinted by permission of Jonathan Cape Ltd.

Lowry, Malcolm, 'Plingen, plangen, aufgefangen' from UNDER THE VOLCANO, Malcolm Lowry, published by Jonathan Cape Ltd. Reprinted by permission of the Executors of the Malcolm Lowry Estate.

MacBeth, George, *Footballer* from COLLECTED POEMS 1958-1970, George MacBeth, 1971, published by Macmillan Ltd. Reprinted by permission of the author.

McGough, Roger, *40-Love* from AFTER THE MERRYMAKING, Roger McGough. Reprinted by permission of Jonathan Cape Ltd.

Marquis, Don, *The Honey Bee* from ARCHY & MEHITABEL. Reprinted by permission of Faber & Faber.

Mayer, Gerda, *The Act, Punch and Judy Show,* from MONKEY ON AN ANALYST'S COUCH, 1980. Reprinted by permission of Ceolfrith Press.

Michie, James, *Dooley is a Traitor* from POSSIBLE LAUGHTER, James Michie. Reprinted by permission of the author.

Mitchell, Adrian, *Now We Are Sick* from FOR BEAUTY DOUGLAS, Adrian Mitchell, 1982. Reprinted by permission of Allison & Busby ltd.

Morgan, Edwin, *The Loch Ness Monster's Song* from FROM GLASGOW TO SATURN, Edwin Morgan. Reprinted by permission of Carcanet New Press.

Morgenstern, Christian, *Fisches Nachtgesang* from ALLE GALGENLIEDER, 1938. Reprinted by permission of Insel Verlag, Frankfurt am Main.

Morton, J.B., *The Borough Councillors Sing to Lady Cabstanleigh* and *Heine* from HERE AND NOW, J.B. Morton, 1937. 'Come hither idiot reader' from HOW TO GROW FLAX. Reprinted by permission of Sheed & Ward Ltd.

Nash, Ogden, *Reply* from HARD LINES, Ogden Nash, published by Simon & Schuster. Reprinted by permission of Curtis Brown Ltd, New York; *Bankers* from I'M A STRANGER HERE MYSELF, Ogden Nash, 1940. Reprinted by permission of Curtis Brown, London, on behalf of the Estate of Ogden Nash.

Parker, Dorothy, *News Item* from THE COLLECTED DOROTHY PARKER, 1965. Reprinted by permision of Gerald Duckworth; *Trinity* from THE RARE ART TRADITIONS, Joseph Alsop, 1982.

Partington, Jonathan R. and a computer, *The Purple Yeti.* Reprinted by permission of the programmer.

Peake, Mervyn, *Aunty Jane, Aunty Vi and Uncle Jake,* from PEAKE'S PROGRESS,1978. Reprinted by permission of Maurice Michael.

Quiller-Couch, Arthur, *The famous Ballad of the Jubilee Cup* **from** STRAW IN THE HAIR, Denys Kilham Roberts, 1938.
© Miss Foy Quiller-Couch

Reading, Peter, *Response* from NOTHING FOR ANYONE, 1977. Reprinted by permission of Martin Secker & Warburg Ltd.

Richardson, Justin, *Vive le Roi* and *High Life Low Down* from VERSE COME, VERSE SERVED, J. Richardson, 1966. Reprinted by permission of Hugh Evelyn Ltd.

Rieu, E.V., *The Happy Hedgehog,* and *The Lady of Leigh* from THE FLATTERED FLYING FISH, E.V. Rieu. Reprinted by permission of Methuen, London.

Scott, F.R. *Brébeuf and his Brethren* from THE COLLECTED POEMS OF F.R. SCOTT. Reprinted by permission of McClelland and Stewart Limited, Toronto, Canada.

Seaman, E. William, *LvB* from JIGGERY-POKERY: A COMPENDIUM OF DOUBLE DACTYLS (ed. Anthony Hecht and John Hollander). © Anthony Hecht and John Hollander. Reprinted with permission of Charles Scribner's Sons.

Sharpless, Stanley J., *Low Church* from THE PENGUIN BOOK OF LIGHT VERSE (ed. Gavin Ewart), 1980 and *Jane* from MINIPOEMS. Reprinted by permission of the author.

Silcock, Ruth, 'When Charles II' from VERSE AND WORSE, (ed. Arnold Silcock), published by Faber & Faber Ltd. Reprinted by permission of the author.

Smith Stevie, *Girls, Autumn, on the Death of a German Philosopher, To the Dog Belvoir, Le Revenant* from THE COLLECTED POEMS OF STEVIE SMITH, published by Allen Lane. Reprinted by permission of James MacGibbon.

Webster, J.J. *The Failure* from FLYOVER 80: THE ANTHOLOGY OF HAMMERSMITH AND FULHAM 1980 FESTIVAL OF POETRY, and *Question and Answer.* Reprinted by permission of the author.

Wells, Carolyn, *The Tutor, Hints on Table Etiquette* from FOLLY FOR THE WISE, Carolyn Wells, 1904, published by Bobbs-Merrill Co Inc, USA.

Wolfe, Humbert, *The Doctor,* from CURSORY RHYMES, 1927; *The Shropshire Lad* from LAMPOONS, 1925. Reprinted by permission of Ann Wolfe.

Wood, Clement Biddle, *Death of a Scrabble Master* from AN ALMANAC OF WORDS AT PLAY (ed. Willard E. Espy). Reprinted by permission of the author.

Woodis, Rodger, *Meaning Business* from THE WOODIS COLLECTION, Rodger Woodis, 1978. Reprinted by permission of Barrie and Jenkins (now part of the Hutchinson Publishing Group).

Wright, Kit, *Sergeant Brown's Parrot* from RABBITING ON, Kit Wright. Reprinted by permission of Fontana Paperbacks.

Yeats, W.B., 'On those who Deal in or who exhibit manuscripts'. Reprinted by permission of Michael and Anne Yeats.

The Editor and Publishers have made every effort to obtain permission for the reproduction of those poems which are in copyright. In one or two cases thry have, however, failed to do so and would be most grateful if they could be informed of what form the acknowledgement should take in future editions of this book.

Books Consulted

Adams, Charles Follen, YAWCOB STRAWS AND OTHER POEMS, 1881.

Allott, Kenneth, SELECTED POEMS OF WINTHROP MACKWORTH PRAED, 1953.

Alsop, Joseph, THE RARE ART TRADITIONS, 1982.

ANTHOLOGIA, 1807.

Baker, Kenneth (ed.) LONDON LINES, 1982.

Bierce, Ambrose, BLACK BEETLES IN AMBER, 1992.

Bishop, Morris, A TREASURY OF BRITISH HUMOUR, 1942.

Boas, Guy (ed.) A SCHOOL BOOK OF LIGHT VERSE, 1945.

Bond, Richmond P., ENGLISH BURLESQUE POETRY, 1932.

Brett, Simon, THE FABER BOOK OF USEFUL VERSE, 1981.

Burgess, Gelett, A GAGE OF YOUTH, 1901.

Carroll, Lewis, THE COLLECTED VERSE OF LEWIS CARROLL, 1932.

Case, A.E., A BIBLIOGRAPHY OF ENGLISH POETICAL MISCELLANIES 1521-1750, 1935.

Cobb, Samuel, POEMS ON SEVERAL OCCASIONS, 1710.

Cohen, J.M., A CHOICE OF COMIC AND CURIOUS VERSE, 1975.

Coleridge, Hartley, POETICAL WORKS.

Cook, Theodore E., AN ANTHOLOGY OF HUMOROUS VERSE, 1906.

Couper, G.W., ORIGINAL POETRY, 1828.

Dobson, Austin, A BOOK-MAN'S BUDGET, 1917.

Ebsworth, J.W. (ed.), MERRY DROLLERY COMPLETE, 1875; WESTMINISTER DROLLERIES, 1875; CHOYCE DROLLERY, 1876.

Elliott, Arthur, THE WITTY AND HUMOROUS SIDE OF THE ENGLISH POETS, 1880.

Espy, Willard R., AN ALMANAC OF WORDS AT PLAY 1957; ANOTHER ALMANAC OF WORDS AT PLAY, 1981.

Ewart, Gavin (ed.), THE PENGUIN BOOK OF LIGHT VERSE, 1980.

Fanshawe, Catherine Maria, THE LITERARY REMAINS OF CATHERINE MARIA FANSHAWE, 1876.

Farley-Hills, David, THE BENEVOLENCE OF LAUGHTER, 1974.

Garrod, Heathcote, EPIGRAMS, 1946.

Godley, A.D., RELIQUIAE, 1926.

Green, Roger, LANCELYN (ed.), A CENTURY OF HUMOROUS VERSE, 1959.

Grigson, Geoffrey, THE FABER BOOK OF NONSENSE VERSE, 1979.

Guiney, Louise Imogen, RECUSANT POETS, 1938.

Halliwell-Phillips, J.O. (ed.), A NORFOLK ANTHOLOGY, 1852.

Halsband, R. and Grundy, I. (ed), ESSAYS AND POEMS BY LADY MARY WORTLEY MONTAGU, 1977.

Harmon, William (ed.) THE OXFORD BOOK OF AMERICAN LIGHT VERSE, 1979.

Henderson, W.B.Drayton (ed.) POEMS FROM PUNCH 1909-1920, 1922.

Huddesford, George, THE POEMS OF GEORGE HUDDESFORD M.A., 1801.

Hunt, Peter (ed.), EATING AND DRINKING, 1961.

Hutchieson, J.C. (ed.), FUGITIVE POETRY 1600-1878, 1878.

Ingrams, Richard (ed.) THE WORKS OF J.B.MORTON, 1974.

Kearney, Patrick, THE PRIVATE CASE, 1981.

King, Ben, BEN KING'S VERSES, 1894.

Knox, E.V. (ed.), HUMOROUS VERSE, 1950.

Langpaap, Frances, THE CATALOG OF THE SCHMULOWITZ COLLECTION OF WIT AND HUMOR, San Francisco Public Library,1962.

Lanigan, George T., PLAY-DAY POEMS, 1879.

LAUGH AND BE FAT, 1733.

Leigh, Henry Sambroke, CAROLS OF COCKAYNE, 1869.

MacKay, Alan L., THE HARVEST OF A QUIET EYE, 1977.

MacKay, L.A., VIPERS BUGLOSS, 1938.

Marcan, Peter, POETRY THEMES, 1977.

THE MERRY-THOUGHT OR, THE GLASS WINDOW AND BOG-HOUSE MISCELLANY, 1732

Morgan, Edward Edwin (ed.), SCOTTISH SATIRICAL VERSE, 1980.

Neaves, Charles (ed.), SONGS AND VERSES: SOCIAL AND SCIENTIFIC, 1878.

Partington, Wilfred (ed.), SMOKE RINGS AND ROUNDELAYS, 1924.

Pope, T. Michael, CAPITAL LEVITIES, 1927 and (ed.) MIDDLESEX IN PROSE AND VERSE, 1930.

Preston, Keith, SPLINTERS, 1921.

Prowse, William Jefferey, NICHOLAS'S NOTES, and SPORTING PROPHECIES, 1870.

Raleigh, Walter, LAUGHTER ON A CLOUD, 1923.

Rankine, W.J.M., SONGS AND FABLES, 1874.

Reilly, Catherine (ed.), SCARS UPON MY HEART, 1981.

Roberts, Denys Kilham (ed.), STRAW IN THE HAIR, 1938.

Robertson of Struan, Alexander, POEMS ON VARIOUS SUBJECTS AND OCCASIONS, Edinburgh.

Scott, R.F. and Smith, A.J.M. (eds), THE BLASTED PINE, 1957.

Silcock, Arnold, VERSE AND WORSE, 1958.

Spurgeon, Caroline, FIVE HUNDRED YEARS OF CHAUCER CRITICISM, 1925.

Stock, Noel, THE LIFE OF EZRA POUND, 1970.

D'Urfey, Thomas, PILLS TO PURGE MELANCHOLY, 1719.

Ward, Ned, THE LONDON SPY, 1709.

Wardroper, John (ed.) LOVE AND DROLLERY, 1969.

Wason, Sandys, MAGENTA MINUTES, 1913.

Wells, Carolyn (ed.) A NONSENSE ANTHOLOGY, 1902 and A PARODY ANTHOLOGY, 1904

Wesley, Samuel, POEMS ON SEVERAL OCCASIONS, 1763.

Wilkinson, C.H. (ed.), DIVERSIONS, 1940 and MORE DIVERSIONS 1843.

Williams, Stephen, and Mortlock, Geoffrey (eds) THE FLOATING BOWL, 1947.

The Decision (p.162), was collected by Miss Jennifer Patterson, and Lines for a Urinal Wall (p.177), by Mr Charles Graham, the editor of Tuba; Meetings (p.107), by Harry Boyle appeared in the Daily Telegraph, November 1981; Moody (p.43), by Thomas Gataker, was reprinted in To-day, Vol 1, 1917, a magazine edited by Holbrook Jackson; The Session of the Poets (p.128), by Robert Buchanan appeared in the Spectator, 15/9/1866; and the first two lines of WLS and EP (p.133), in the New Yorker, 1/1/1938. Kabocha Gennari (p.132), is a Japanese poet whose name means 'Fed Up With Pumpkins'.

Index

The night was growing old
  As she trudged through snow and sleet;
And her nose was long and cold,
  And her shoes were full of feet.

ANONYMOUS

The Played out Humourist